Write The Vision Creative Works

BROKEN LEADER

CALLING ALL LEADERS:
STOP HIDING BEHIND
PAST PAIN

VALENCYA THOMPSON

Write The Vision Creative Works,LLC

Broken Leader

Write The Vision Creative Works, LLC

Writethevisioncreativeworks.com

Copyright © 2022 by Valencya Thompson.
All rights reserved. Printed in the United States of America. No portion of this book may be reproduced, stored in a retrieval system or transmitted in any form or by any means, electronic, mechanical, photocopying, recording or otherwise without the prior permission of the copyright owner. Requests should be addressed to Valencya Thompson at cew@writethevisioncreativeworks.com. Visit brokenleader-book.com for author updates. Scripture quotations are from New Revised Standard Version Bible, copyright © 1989 National Council of the Churches of Christ in the United States of America. Used by permission. All rights reserved worldwide. Scripture quotations taken from The Holy Bible, New International Version® NIV® Copyright © 1973 1978 1984 2011 by Biblica, Inc. TM Used by permission. All rights reserved worldwide.
Cover Design & Interior Formatting: Valencya Thompson
Editing: ADM Agency - Michaela Carter
Photo used on Cover - Andrew Burgess - stock.adobe.com
Library of Congress Control Number:

2022930206

Printed in USA

Dedicated to

Justice, Broughton & Josiah.

Never shrink. Walk tall

and fully as God created you.

Contents

Foreword – Jason Bates iv

Prologue – Me & The Birds 9

STEP I

Understanding Your Broken Reality

– An Introduction 15

STEP II

The Assessment - Isolating What Broke You . . . 25

STEP III

Cracked Identity

– Locating the Basis for Your Second-Guessing . . 35

STEP IV

Broken Hope

– The Remedy for Your Kryptonite 45

STEP V

Brokenness

– See the Label to Remove the Label 55

STEP VI

Gracefully Broken

– Realizing God Uses It All 63

STEP VII

Beyond Repair

– Can I Be Put Back Together Again? 77

STEP VIII

Getting in Touch with Who God Says You Are So You Can Embrace

Change And Be Who You Are 87

STEP IX

Being Beyond Recognition is A Good Thing Because God

is Doing A New Thing 95

STEP X

Ten Habits to Help You Embrace Loving Your New Reflection

. 105

EPILOGUE

Holding Onto A Promise 111

ACKNOWLEDGMENTS 113

Broken Leaders experience hardships, go through self-doubt, question what they know God has purposed them to do. Broken Leaders often have their trust dismantled. All the while, they are still capable of impacting and inspiring others. Broken Leaders are powerful. Broken Leaders are resilient. If it's in you, no matter the failures or what may seem like failures in the natural, you still have to get back up. You will experience some hard things, but success comes from pruning. This provides expertise for the work God has called your hands to touch. If you were not a Broken Leader, you would not possess the grit to push harder to be the leader you're called to be. You may question your education level. People around you may even question what God has put in you. Still, God will allow your works, talents, and education to shine through. God will allow those around you who have questioned (silently or publicly) your process to begin to see God's hand on your life. No matter what negative thoughts, words, or anything contrary to the Spirit of God in you arise; always remember, you possess the positivity within you to combat them. Even if negative thoughts appear in your nightly dreams, the good within will conquer them. God's strength within you will crush every opposing force. Leader, you can do this!

- Jason Bates

PROLOGUE:
Me & The Birds

When this Prologue was written, I was seated at my kitchen table with my left foot broken in three places. This was due to an injury sustained from passing out in my hallway and hitting my foot on the doorframe on the way down. My body desperately panted for air as I realized I had lost my sense of smell. I was sure I had contracted the COVID-19 virus. I would soon learn my assumption was correct. And despite the EMTs who arrived with the ambulance diagnosing me as I lay on the floor, I knew better. They assuredly stated, "Well, your foot's not broken, and if you have COVID, there is no point in going to the ER because they're probably not going to do anything for you, so you wanna get up off the floor and stay home?" Thankfully I heard the still small voice say, "Go to the hospital."

Once admitted, I was treated there for two nights and three days. I was also diagnosed with double pneumonia. Discharged after 7:00 p.m. Sent home without pain medication, as the only open pharmacist nearby didn't have my prescription in stock. Back home, the Lord began to speak. He let me know my present crushing was due to me sitting on a few things for some years due to fear. This book is one of them. God let me know in God's own way He was sick of my foolishness, and it was time to go to work. So here we are.

Prayerfully, you can learn from my testimony and avoid having a similar unnecessary experience. One of the toughest things about enduring this circumstance was the period of isolation. Understand, God will isolate you from people and your routine to get your attention. Again, I hope and pray in your reading the sharing of my account, you can avoid having to go through it yourself. Our family worked together to evacuate our children from the home as my husband, Jerrell, was also diagnosed with coronavirus. I repeated (*when I could talk*) to everyone who would listen; it felt like our children were sucked up in a vacuum, almost like they were never here. With my eldest being nearly seven and us not being away from our children longer than three nights before, it was a surreal experience for them to be gone for two weeks. My husband slept upstairs in our bedroom as I slept downstairs in the family room - in the bed he pushed through to set up for me despite battling his illness. I questioned in moments when my sickness was getting the best of me if my children were ever here, as my new companions became a bedside commode, wheelchair, and walker.

Jerrell was stronger than me – or his strong will enabled him to present himself as such. He was the sole caretaker of us both. The house was very quiet. Well, except for the birds. But I'll get to them in a moment. And as the eldest of the millennials, I imagined myself, more than once, rapping *Through the Wire* like Kanye while the Holy Spirit downloaded messages as I recovered. Except my wire looked a little different.

Falling backward was what the dream revealed. God gave my aunt and me the same dream as a warning about a month or two before this setback. It came along with a promise. The promise was God would be with me. My isolation period began in the hospital – as no one can be with you, and there are no visitors allowed when hospitalized with COVID. I immediately felt the spiritual and mental battle happening, with the physical just at the surface. I was in a literal fight for my life! The fight was to live as I never had! To live beyond fear! Just as in this illness, we may battle feelings of loneliness and isolation under other circumstances. Along with feeling no one else understands unless they too have gone through it.

Crushing. Breaking.

So, about those birds. There were birds in my chimney when I resided in the family room during my illness. The fireplace was just a few feet over from the foot of the bed I slept in. After a bit of research, Jerrell let me know the birds are called chimney swifts. And, of course, the Holy Spirit let me know the birds were here for me. So, here's the message. *Birds fly after brokenness.*

Chimney swifts are born *blind. Fragile. Weak. Vulnerable. Dependent* upon parents to come back and feed them as they rest inside the chimney. They are stuck in a nest and can do nothing except *try* to grow as they endure this new process of life. They rest in darkness. In the chimney, chirping, building muscle. *Learning* to flap their wings. <u>In the dark.</u> They are blind and blind in the dark. Does simultaneously experiencing both matter? *Blindness and darkness?* Are the birds aware? Yes, it matters! Because the darkness shields them. The darkness protects them. It hides them from predators in the world while they are still in the most vulnerable state - **new, novice. Untainted. Inexperienced. Unfamiliar with the dangers of the world.**

I'm reminded of another facet of my temporary circumstance. Don't get COVID-19 with injuries. Until COVID-free, or in my case, COVID plus bilateral pneumonia-free, treatment may be delayed in other areas. While the hospital did provide a splint, I was told to stay off my foot without much further direction. However, I am truly thankful for the physical therapist and occupational therapist who came to teach me how to use my walker and hop on one foot safely!

The orthopedist on-call advised, "Since feet are not my specialty and because you have insurance, I'll refer you to see my colleague once discharged." You can imagine my dismay as I was on a three-way call with my sorority sister,

Candice. She acted as my voice when I heard the orthopedic office staff advise nothing would be done for my foot until I was free of COVID. My appointment had to be scheduled a minimum of two weeks post being discharged from the hospital. Trust, I understand the rationale during a pandemic from a medical and practical place, but this is separate from my human feelings and never experiencing broken bones before. But there I was. I was terrified my foot could be further damaged. So, mostly (*except a few moments of rare strong-willed insanity*), I did everything I could to protect my foot and stay off it. My wonderful husband also went above and beyond to protect my foot. Jerrell took care of me in ways I don't desire to describe. To acknowledge we are both human, I will mention we had a few task-focused spats here and there.

    We *protected* so well until I arrived at my orthopedic appointment, and I was advised my bones were healing (*even if slowly*). Even if it could take up to six months to heal completely. I was thankful to know I hadn't caused any further damage. This kind of protection can be likened to how the birds were protected in the chimney— protected while in their broken, fragile, underdeveloped state provided a safe place for them to grow and even heal. And just as the adult birds were there, even after gathering food, God is. The sweet physical therapist from the hospital, a middle-aged White lady, chuckled as she introduced herself to me. "My name is Karen, but I promise I don't act like that." Karen overheard my struggles as a hospitalized vegan and offered to bring me food the next morning. Would you know she purchased an entire bag of vegan goodies and even whipped me up a large batch of my favorite, JUST Egg? When I could eat, I craved JUST Egg for some reason throughout my entire recovery process. Karen's kindness, along with several others who provided great care, were all my reminder: God was with me, just as promised.

    Untainted. Inexperienced. Unfamiliar with the dangers of the world. Yet they chirp! They practice! Day and night! They get their vocals right! Because in the future their song is of the utmost importance! Their song and their flight are the purpose. Their song reminds you to wake up, get going, persevere! Their flight, which took weeks to build enough strength in their fragile new bodies to even dare to attempt, reminds you of the most significant and critical calling to fulfill in life, TAKE OFF! It's what God has always wanted and what He requires at this time.

I said I wanted to work out my arms. Using a wheelchair isn't exactly what I had in mind, but there I was anyway. Who would've known *the breaking could be beautiful?* Come on out, little birdie. It's okay. The big beautiful blue sky awaits you!

The opportunity of brokenness can provide a multitude of benefits. For example, in my temporary disability, I quickly processed through my groanings what was most disruptive, the learning curve! There was a learning curve for everything! And imagine being forced to learn in a course you never signed up for, let alone weren't interested in. And the course material was required to graduate in your major. A disability due to a new injury forces you to utilize muscles you never use (or use less frequently). You're also forced to use these less frequently used muscles in unconventional ways or ways novel to you.

This phenomenon can be likened to going back into the gym after being out of shape for quite some time. You hit the mat and go hard on Day One, only to be sore the next day - and you feel pain in places you didn't know muscles dwelled. Fitness trainers typically encourage you to work out different muscles on different days. One, to avoid muscle memory, and two, to prevent overuse or hurting yourself unnecessarily.

With an injury, you are now forced to continue using new muscles in new ways, and you must do so strategically to avoid further damage. But it hurts. Like legit, my entire body is aching now simply because of me working to transition my body from place to place without plopping down. This requires core strength. Which ashamedly, I don't have a lot of at the moment. Albeit micro, muscles must tear to grow. If you're feeling a bit torn up and even broken, realize growth is next.

What if, just what if, after your opportunity of brokenness, all the weak places were made stronger? What if, just what if, you discover you have a core after all? What if, just what if, you begin to discern with keen awareness how to move in all those weak spots with agility? In ways you never imagined for yourself before. It is time to unleash God's greatness within! Do not let your pain be for naught. The painful experience was never intended to cripple you indefinitely. It has always had an expiry point. The painful experience is intended to catapult you into destiny. It is now time to be launched! Now fly!

STEP ONE:
Understanding Your Broken Reality - An Introduction

Devotional

Romans 8.33-39 NRSV -

Who will bring any charge against God's elect? It is God who justifies. Who is to condemn? Is it Christ Jesus, who died, yes, who was raised, who is at the right hand of God, who indeed intercedes for us. Who will separate us from the love of Christ? Will hardship, or distress, or persecution, or famine, or nakedness, or peril, or sword? As it is written, 'For your sake we are being killed all day long; we are accounted as sheep to be slaughtered.' No, in all these things, we are more than conquerors through him who loved us. For I am convinced that neither death, nor life, nor angels, nor rulers, nor things present, nor things to come, nor powers, nor height, nor depth, nor anything else in all creation, will be able to separate us from the love of God in Christ Jesus our Lord.

This scripture is powerful, scary, intimidating, and empowering all at the same time. Many of us have been charged and condemned while on a path to purpose. And while it is refreshing to know Christ Jesus died for us and is currently interceding on our behalf at the right hand of God, life can be troublesome. We are very easily blinded by past hurts, present pain, and future magnification of our fears by the adversary during various seasons. If any of this sounds like what you've experienced in your life, then you, my friend, might be a Broken Leader.

We've all been broken at one time or another. The question arises, "Can we identify our brokenness?" Especially when the thing(s) that broke us happened a while back. Especially when we have barricaded the memory of them in the deepest darkest caverns of our minds. Beyond our subconscious. Nearly to the point of unconsciousness. In the depths of our souls. In locations unbeknownst to us. Despite our efforts, there is some hurt we simply cannot hide. Even our souls feel the residual pain. Could there be a permanent chip on your shoulder? Is there a buzz going around? Bzzzz. Are friends and family saying you need to "just get over it?" Hmmm.

Were your talents visible at an early age? Did your parents or guardians predict you would become successful at one specific thing? And, to your disappointment, your dream deferred, your wait, or your wilderness period brought you to a point where you crashed down to your knees? Some might say, "You are stuck." For some reason, you can't seem to dig yourself out the mud. Here lies the issue. Perhaps God doesn't want you to dig yourself out! Maybe God is prepared, equipped, and more than able to save you without your help. For it is Jesus, alone, who saves us all. Acknowledge you are stuck. Then, and only then, God might position you in the trenches to do the work. To climb out. To understand your broken reality.

I am so glad you picked up this book! My quest is to help you dig a little deeper into the places you have ignored and have hoped to escape. To help you conquer your past hurt and pain. You have been broken. And in some instances, for far too long. Yes, God has allowed it. And none of us want to hear that. But your brokenness is all for His Glory. Remember, Romans 8:28 NRSV, "We know that all things work together for good for those who love God, who are called according to his purpose." And yes, this moment of hurt that you can't seem to push past is a part of the *all* referenced in the scripture. Broken, yes. Permanent, no. He never intended for you to stay there. It's time for you to let go of the wilderness. Yes, there were certain things you had to do to survive, but now you are past that point. God has your breakthrough right in His hands, and right on the other side of breakthrough is manifestation. But it will require your trust. Trust me, God's hand is extended to you even now. Now is your time. Reach out and grab it!

A Peek through My Window

My family endured four and a half years of financial hardship. Forced into full-time entrepreneurship while grieving previous losses, with two of my children born into the world. Reaching a point of feeling the bottom was just about to fall out, emotions at an all-time high, fires inside my heart, and even one in my driveway (*yes, a car really caught fire in my driveway*). Change was knocking at my door!

No longer could we rely solely on book publishing and editing clients who come and go in waves or the next magazine client; it was time for something I fought for so long. It was time to pursue another nine to five. Thankfully, my husband, Jerrell, has always been stable in his career, so we had a consistent paycheck, but it required more for us to live. I did what any other reasonable adult would; I pulled out my grown woman strength and reached out to my network to find a job. I attached it to a prayer, "Lord, this job cannot be a departure from the things you have called me to do; it must add to them!" By God's grace and a wonderful sorority sister, I soon landed a position.

The hourly gig would last three months, but it provided a consistent paycheck for my financial contribution to our home. We could catch up on daycare fees and our mortgage. The cherry on top, those who worked there said, "If you want a permanent job, you can have one." With God's prompt, "You are here to learn," in mind, I had no idea how long I would remain at this educational pit stop, but I took it seriously and worked hard to excel in my temporary role. This was easy for me as the temporary position allowed me to work in my element! I traveled from company to company and spoke before audiences! I shared moving stories with the hearts of listeners and compelled them to give. This came to me naturally. I have a heart of compassion, and public speaking is something I enjoy!

As time moved on, the honeymoon phase subsided. The veil lifted, and I learned more behind-the-scenes. I learned how my experience was not common among my peers. I had a nice set-up, but my colleagues did not. I eventually noticed all things didn't align. I knew my God said He brought me there to learn, so I chose to follow the path until God told me otherwise.

Towards the end of my term, I scheduled meetings with permanent employees, with whom I developed rapport and somewhat trusted. I gleaned from their insight and positioned myself to be a standout candidate for a permanent position. To my dismay, there was no permanent position which would afford me the same opportunities I enjoyed while temporary. Yet, I stayed the course for God and my family. I applied with the marketing department and others for writing opportunities. I didn't hear back quickly, so I opted for the low-hanging fruit. I applied for and accepted a permanent position within the department I worked for temporarily. Though, I was highly skeptical. I would report to someone who was a company veteran but new to supervising others. Who reported to my, then, current supervisor and was preceded by a negative reputation. I distrusted I would be objectively evaluated as successful in the position for many reasons. The position previously reported to someone else who remained within the company—the former employee in the role left by choice. The company purposely changed the title of the position and removed many responsibilities, seemingly selling it in a lower pay tier. The adapted role was placed in the hands of a supervisor admittingly clueless to what the job would entail, whose supervisor also had no clue what to do with it. What does this sound like? A disaster! Yes! It was the perfect set-up for my downfall. But like I said, I opted for the low-hanging fruit. I needed a consistent paycheck.

    I found myself reporting to two individuals who changed their directives as quickly as the wind blew and who had no problem throwing others under the bus to save themselves. There was no proper onboarding – a company flaw. There was no real training. They were plagued with amnesia as it suited them, and it was evident, no one in a position of power was in my corner. I sought advice from others, but the resounding word was it was a workplace where different rules and standards applied to different people. Unfortunately, there was a disproportionate number of unfavorable factors towards African American employees. And worst, our department was known for making a target out of intelligent African American women. What a precarious position to be in!

    I questioned my ability to endure. Physically. Mentally. Emotionally. *Old school* tells us we are blessed to work inside air-conditioned offices, which our degrees afforded us. But *New school* confirms though we have made generational strides, there is still much more work to be done for our societal advancement. Add to this, my temporary position ended in December. I started the permanent position the same month and learned the prophecy was revealed! I was pregnant with my third child, who would survive after we endured several miscarriages. I have physical limitations which accompany my pregnancies. The job granted remote privileges, but it was up to the supervisor's discretion. After a long delay, I was granted one day of remote privileges after working for nearly four months in my permanent role. Finances from this position coupled with gracious donations allowed me to host my first Fertility Hope Women's Conference. God assigned this to my heart the June before my employment. Revenue for prenatal appointments was available.

This was an answer. Over a year prior, when God had our closest friends tell us a third baby was on the way, my first question was, "How will we pay for it?" *This was honest. Human. Instinctual.*

New Year's Eve night, I was contacted online by a major ghostwriter seeking assistance. He and I met face-to-face New Year's Day, where he explicitly explained what he was looking for in a writer. He stated, "It is not difficult to find talented writers, they are everywhere, but a teachable writer is what I need." He introduced me to a new writing style adopted by major publishers. He explained, "They would never tell you what you don't have, just, 'You don't have it,' as they look past you." Turns out there is a certain flavor, yes, the *juice or sauce* in any industry! He also made it clear if our writing relationship didn't work, he would thank me, and we would quickly part ways. I left his office completely positively overwhelmed by all he taught me! Just the view from the top of the Buckhead skyline his office overlooked did it for me. And I thought to myself, "Even if he doesn't hire me, I am truly thankful just for our encounter." He was the *Millionaire Ghostwriter*! Someone who accomplished what I was and still dream of achieving.

Thankfully, he saw me ready for the next level and hired me for contract work as needed. I was paid more than I ever have been paid before with any other writing gig! *Pregnant.* Still working a nine to five with a demanding supervisor. Coming home to nurture my husband and two children. Trying to write to meet the ghostwriter's deadlines. In the car on the way to work and after as Jerrell drove. All while planning our first conference and trying to keep everything else at bay! Imagine me feeling like I was trying to catch a sip from a fire hydrant! I thought, "Wow! God, you must really trust me!" I told the ghostwriter I found it hilarious when I had more availability, we hadn't met yet. It would be when I was trying to manage a full plate, the opportunities would come. This, my friends, is called life.

I was praising God the conference manifested just as He promised. It was beautiful! It stretched our faith, those who helped, and those who attended in more ways than we could count. I see the residual effects now two years later. A few weeks before the conference, things had gotten better between my supervisor and me.

Ebbs and flows.

The moment I returned to work, I was placed in the fiery furnace! It would be exactly one month following the conference when I would be released from my job. While things felt tumultuous, and I had plans to walk out during my maternity leave, I was still shocked. And though there was no job security because I was with the company less than a year, I was blind-sided. I didn't see the termination coming. But in true fashion, the Holy Spirit let me know, despite any wrong-doing I felt or what friends around me witnessed, "I didn't have time to look back; there was too much work for me to do!" I was provided a timely break from contracting with the ghostwriter as the conference season approached.

Exactly two weeks before the nine to five was snatched away, God flooded me with contracts for my business. I spoke on a panel during a motherhood brunch two weeks post my conference, and a friend of the host heard I was a ghostwriter and book publisher. Her book is now published. Additional prospects found me via my website and are now published. And in God's wisdom, when I was hired by the nine to five, I also accepted a contract position with another company for part-time work. All these things would be the exact opportunities sustaining our family during the next shift. Multiple streams. Understand this season also had its own set of trials, but we were covered. In this week's counseling session, my counselor said to me, "Where does the Bible say trusting God means our lives will be without trials?" I responded, "Nowhere," and I was right.

As I had done with my other two babies who survived the womb, I would be afforded the opportunity to work full-time from home, using my God-given talents and hone my craft even more! I was truly thankful! But, as *a true broken leader*, I also had my doubts. Some days I was up, working well, fully believing the promises of God, and other days, I agreed with the lies the enemy would tell me. "Perhaps, I'm the problem." "Maybe, I have difficulty reporting to others." "What's wrong with me?" "Why can't I keep a nine to five like everyone else?"

Lies. Lies. Lies.

I'm sure you've heard them too! Perhaps, you were created for another purpose! Perhaps, God created some to support someone else's vision, and others were called to create a vision!

You are not wrong.

You heard God correctly.

Yes, we do supplement the vision and even fund it at times, through working for and with others, in and out of seasons, but never are we ever to put down the mantle God has given us. Always remember, God is your source. God is THE SOURCE. Keep going. You were born to lead!

Pray This:

Dear Heavenly Father:

Thank You for allowing me to see my brokenness and accept it. Thank You for loving me in spite of the battle I have been in with You over releasing it all to You. Please forgive me for my words saying, "I trust," when my actions don't align. Help me to be a hypocrite no more. Allow me to fully trust You to take all the broken pieces and make me whole again. In Jesus' Name, I pray. Amen.

CONGRATULATIONS ON COMPLETING STEP ONE! IF YOU HAVE THE MIRROR CLEANING STUDY GUIDE, HEAD ON OVER AND READ THE FIRST EXERCISE. YOU ARE ONE STEP CLOSER TO YOUR BREAKTHROUGH!

STEP TWO:

The Assessment – Isolating What Broke You

Devotional

Romans 8.1-4 NRSV -

There is; therefore, now no condemnation for those who are in Christ Jesus. For the law of the Spirit of life in Christ Jesus has set you free from the law of sin and of death. For God has done what the law, weakened by the flesh, could not do: by sending his own Son in the likeness of sinful flesh, and to deal with sin, he condemned sin in the flesh, so that the just requirement of the law might be fulfilled in us, who walk not according to the flesh but according to the Spirit.

Have you ever been subjected to the authority of individuals who possessed no leadership skills? As in placed in a position above your position, but frankly, they were completely out of position? We find, in such moments, incubators for frustration, manipulation, hidden agendas, workplace/work-related conflict, and more. It is in such moments where you realize your reality: you are a leader. You were born to lead! It is in such moments you will learn to be led by the Spirit and not the flesh. And, if you follow suit, you will isolate what broke you.

Albeit painful to listen to ill-fitted recommendations from a demanding supervisor, it is in moments like these where you become familiar with the leader within. You hear your inner voice constantly proposing alternatives to what is being suggested before you. And if you dare share any of your proposals aloud, they will be shot down. You'll soon recognize you are not the captain of the ship you are currently voyaging upon. Could it be God has positioned you here, not to torment you, but instead to develop you? Yes – you, my friend, have been brought to this place in life for one primary reason: to learn! Let's not jump to any conclusions. You cannot put a time stamp on how long you will dwell in this place. All I can tell you is you should focus on your lesson through constant communion with the Holy Spirit and ask the right questions daily. "Father, will You please help me to see what it is You desire for me to see in this place?" "Father, will You please help me to not miss out on learning what You sent me here to learn?" "Holy Spirit, will You please dwell and abide with me every day and help me to discern what I must, during this season?" "Father, I plead the blood of Jesus over my life and over all You have given me charge of as I plant my feet one in front of the other to complete these tasks you've set before me." "Please walk with me." "Please walk ahead of me." "I promise, I will follow as you lead."

In submission to an ill-fitted authority figure, your triggers will be made apparent to you. You will come to know what ticks you have, and more importantly, if you choose to, you will begin to identify and eventually isolate what broke you. As in, what brought the chip on your shoulder. How'd you get that little snag on your sweater? Why does it pull more whenever you're in a prickly situation?

You will isolate it, and this will prepare you for the next phase of work to begin. Do not be afraid, instead ask God for help! Use your wherewithal to maneuver and allow the Holy Spirit to be your constant guide. Resist the urge to lean on your own understanding and always remember God knows best. Walk in the Spirit, not in the flesh.

It is necessary to go back to the place where you were broken. This is where you can take back your power, where you regain control, and where you reject fear so it can return to hell – its origin. For some, a physical return is not necessary, nor is it beneficial. If this applies to you, ground yourself in the mental and spiritual work of looking back. Process. Undergo internal reflection. And for others, a physical return is required. If this is for you, you will know. Just be sure to check The Spirit, discern, and confirm in Jesus' name. The exodus must take place at the breaking point. It is where you will find the entry point for your new season. There you will be able to open the door and walk right through, but first, you must go back and complete your work.

A Peek through My Window

I often refer to myself as a recovering people-pleaser. Old friends know why. Fraught with searching for my father's love and misinterpretation of Christianity as a youth, I wanted to be liked. And I wanted to be liked by everyone! So, I did everything within my power to make myself desirable to others. I wanted my teachers to like me. I wanted everyone to be my friend. I prided myself in conflict resolution and seeing the least of these. My skewed perception followed me well into young adulthood and seeps out occasionally even now. Vying for the attention of teachers and friends translated into vying for the approval of employers/supervisors/clients and colleagues professionally and family/friends socially.

I indirectly learned to be deemed a righteous Christian, it would be best for me to put myself last.

A desire to not be *selfish* + wanting to be seen as <u>selfless</u> = self-last.

Self-last. Have you ever found yourself here? And worse, positioned there by your own design? Since when did burning the candle at both ends and neglecting self become desirable traits? When did denying self-care become admirable? As the adage says, "you cannot pour from an empty cup." Lord knows I've had to learn this the hard way. Cloud & Townsend say it this way in *Boundaries*, "Workers who continually take on duties that aren't theirs will eventually burn out. It takes wisdom to know what we should be doing and what we shouldn't. We can't do everything."

Fear of rejection is the precursor to *self-last*. Be honest. No one wants to be rejected, and many have gone to great lengths to avoid it, but it happens. By design, everyone will not like you. The key is not to take it personally. God created a big world full of many people of diverse cultures with various talents and skillsets. He poured gifts out without consideration of specific groups of people only being eligible for receiving them. We have different interests and different attractions. Consequently, we are repelled by certain things that others may be drawn towards. This includes personality types.

Still, there are times when what you are initially attracted to can become something (*or someone*) you are repelled by over time. This is the result of many factors, but now we will address two: *presentation* and *progression*.

Constructs Defined:

Presentation – The art of presenting *your idea* of your <u>best self</u> or who you strive to be and *deem desirable* to others at first meeting. You attempt to maintain this persona as time passes in your relationships with others, but glimpses of your true self gradually surface. Like all charades, this phenomenon is a temporary state.

Progression – You have previously introduced your authentic self to those you have grown in close relationship with, but you are changing. If this change is healthy and propels you to fulfill God's purpose(s) for your life, you are in this state.

Presentation mode is a false reality. And while most never intend to end up here, it happens to many. A *recovering people-pleaser* will start a relationship with an impossible pretense, to become the "be-all and end-all" for someone else. You start by saying "yes" to every request. You even infringe on prior engagements established by your immediate family – which should be your first ministry. You've poured out so much that your cup is empty. Instead of thinking to stop and get a refill, you keep pouring. *It's all air!* It's as insane as driving a car for several miles on empty with the gas indicator lit, and you willingly pass by several gas stations. Even though there is enough money in your bank account to fill your tank, you keep driving. It is time to refuel! Your engine is strained by the lack of proper maintenance and care. If you don't stop now, the damage will become irreparable ... *or will it?*

Yes, God is sovereign, and the Psalms tell us God is even with us in the depths of hell (139:8), but there are always repercussions, consequences, and reactions to the choices we make in life. Thankfully, God's grace and mercy can restore us; however, we cannot un-experience what we have experienced. Some experiences sharpen us, and some show us grace. Both are designed to show us the nature of God.

Progression mode is the healthier place to be. It can feel lonely and often leave one feeling misunderstood, but this comes along frequently on the road less traveled. There are many things we cannot know, and surely, we do not know the mind of God. Yet, the scriptures tell us if we call out to God, God will answer us and tell us things we cannot know (Jeremiah 33:3). One thing is certain, God did not place any of us within the earth so we might remain the same. Life is full of transition. Just as sure as we become accustomed to one way of doing things, our situations change. It's time to learn a new way!

As a matter of fact, this chapter is being written amid the Covid-19 pandemic. Who knew in this lifetime, year 2020, we would advance beyond understanding the word *epi*demic to *pan*demic? Who knew, but God, life as we knew it would forever be impacted, seemingly overnight?

I am a hugger. I am known for hugging people upon arrival and departure. I kiss cheeks, I hold babies, I enjoy a good laugh with a friend over a meal and drinks. I am an extrovert (*mostly*). I draw energy from being around others – especially on a down day. Now forced to conduct business and socialize remotely – seemingly, we are all living in a new day. Reminiscent of another time and place. Change. It happens. Whether we are willing participants or not.

Let's bring this home. How do individuals who have been friends for an extensive amount of time, who've shared secrets and become close confidantes just stop being friends? It's not simple, and there is no easy answer. Somehow the repelling process starts. After many years of suffering, one friend (*Friend A*) could be in a season of receiving answered prayers from God. The other (*Friend B*) could have prayed alongside Friend A during prior seasons; yet, once the very prayers come to pass for Friend A, Friend B is so blinded by her own pain, Friend B is unwilling to be supportive any longer. On the surface, this can appear to be jealousy *(and in some cases, it is)*. On a deeper level, Friend B has not yet properly harnessed the spiritual tools our heavenly Father has granted for us to grasp. These tools help us see beyond the natural (*present pain*) and celebrate those we love, despite our own setbacks. It takes spiritual maturity to understand how to wield such tools. One such tool is understanding the power of testimony. There are many accounts in The Word of God in support of sharing our testimonies. Here are a few:

1) *Jesus did not let him, but said, "Go home to your own people and tell them how much the Lord has done for you, and how he has had mercy on you"* (Mark 5:19 NIV).

2) *Come and hear, all you who fear God; let me tell you what he has done for me* (Psalm 66:16 NIV).

3) *And let us consider how we may spur one another on toward love and good deeds, not giving up meeting together, as some are in the habit of doing, but encouraging one another—and all the more as you see the Day approaching* (Hebrews 10:24-25 NIV).

The unfortunate part about friendships which dissolve during seasons like referenced above is God made relationships cyclical by design. When one is down, and the other is up, she can build up the other and vice versa (Ecclesiastes 4:10).

No one wants to be fully absorbed by any other person.

– Gloria Ketter

Let's unpack this statement by one of my spiritual mothers. The conversation was about my not receiving the desired response from my primarily introverted husband, contrarily to my extroverted self – amid quarantine. It did not dawn on me until this conversation, I was treating my husband in the same manner I avoid having others treat me.

Such a conundrum.

While resting in my desire to not be controlled, I was attempting to control him.

This was wrong.

The same is true on the other side of the equation. It is unfair to yourself and others to falsely presume you can be everything to anyone else. Where is the room for God in this? Furthermore, it is quite characteristic of a *god complex* to think this is even possible, especially encapsulated in our humanity. What is the origin of your brokenness? How exactly did you get here? How can you isolate what happened in the past to discern what God is doing in your present?

Walk not according to the flesh but according to the Spirit.

When you do, you are creating a space for The Holy Spirit to lead and touch the tender places of your heart. Then, God can mend the brokenness.

Pray This:

Dear Heavenly Father:

Please help me to transition from *Presentation* to *Progression* in my relationships. Allow me to mature more so I may better establish boundaries in all areas. Help me understand the difference between being the Believer You called me to be versus the one made up by the world. Then, please help me to walk in it every day. Thank You, Most Gracious Father, for hearing my prayer. In Jesus' Name, I pray. Amen.

WHEW! YOU HAVE COMPLETED STEP TWO! I LOOK FORWARD TO JOINING YOU OVER IN THE MIRROR CLEANING STUDY GUIDE FOR THE SECOND EXERCISE REMEMBER, YOU'VE GOT THIS! EVEN BETTER, GOD DOES.

STEP THREE: Cracked Identity – Locating the Basis for Your Second-Guessing

Devotional

Romans 8.5-6 NRSV –

For those who live according to the flesh set their minds on the things of the flesh, but those who live according to the Spirit set their minds on the things of the Spirit. To set the mind on the flesh is death, but to set the mind on the Spirit is life and peace.

Cracked.

One day my husband, Jerrell, and I were riding down the highway near a golf course, and a golf ball smashed into the windshield out of nowhere!

It formed a perfect little crack.

I was terrified as it struck the front passenger side. I wasn't sure what hit us at the moment, but thankfully it didn't penetrate beneath the surface of the glass. We were left with *permanent brokenness*, visible to all who saw our truck. We didn't get it repaired. So, it spread. Before we knew it, a tiny problem had grown to be an even bigger problem. It caused me to second-guess driving it to certain appointments. First, because of fear of it breaking and causing harm. Second, because of what people might say or think. For a little while, it was a trigger for me as I braced myself for family and friends' commentary when we pulled up. After a while, this stopped, and the cracked glass became a part of our vehicular *identity*. I didn't even think of the cracks specifically anymore. I just knew I loathed the look of the vehicle – though it still reliably gets us around.

Just like our cracked glass, your identity can become cracked after seasons of pain. Pain is a part of process. Anyone called to leadership is no stranger to affliction. A great leader is taught through experience, mentorship, and by *Spirit*. With Holy Bible in hand, and a promise to follow God in your heart, tough times still come. And after a while, big faith may feel as though it has dwindled to the size of a mustard seed. Thankfully, scripture tells us mustard seed faith is all it takes to move mountains (Matt 17:20)! But what if the mountain obstructs your heart?

Some experiences leave behind God-sized holes.

-Rev. Kendra Ketter Chavis

No matter the situation or circumstance, God is enough. You must choose to allow God to point you towards the origin of your cracked identity so you can stop your second-guessing! No matter how broken your situation or how broken you may feel. No matter how tiny the cracks or how many, God can repair your heart, and God can heal you from the pain of your past. It's time to get out your head. It's time to no longer walk by flesh. It's time to let the Spirit guide.

A Peek through My Window

The body does what the body does.

– Ruth Ubaldo

The above quotation is from my spiritual Sister. She shared these words while encouraging me during my season of miscarriages. Though my husband and I have since birthed three healthy children in the world, we have lost four babies for heaven's gain. You may read about this specific testimony in a book authored by my husband, Jerrell, and myself, *Our Journey to #fertilityhope*. For the present purpose, I am referencing my season of miscarriages to share what I have gleaned from the experience.

Discovery: Doing good will not keep you from hurting bad.

Hmm. Well, this is terrible. Surely, at some point or another, you've hoped your good deeds might deem you good and exempt you from hurt. They do not. Your reading this book is evidence of you being experienced in living, so I'm willing to make an educated guess and say you already knew this. Still, it hasn't kept you from hoping this from time to time. Think on the hymn often quoted in obituaries, "May the Work I've Done Speak for Me."[1] And while, I too, hope my character and integrity are seen by those who know me, fact is – we are guaranteed to experience joy and trials while here.

Feeling lost from God during trauma happens.

Yes, indeed, it happens to the best of us. And the worst thing to occur during one of these seasons (*or so it seems at the time*) is for a Bible-thumper to throw scripture at you without consideration of your context. For you too, who might be able to rightly divide the Word just as well as any other exegetist, may know what it's like to hurt so badly and feel numb. You may have cried so many tears until you feel you can't cry *one* more. It is in times like these where you must tap into the strength of your loved ones. Not just any. Those who know how to call on the name of Jesus and how to usher in the presence of God. Those who know how to worship *for you* when your well has run dry. Those who know how to go to war when you feel too beaten to go to battle for yourself. The power of intercession is a spiritual weapon of immense importance. But for some, when your identity is cracked, you second-guess who to trust. You may even find yourself in a state of paranoia. Scary stuff. Yes! I know.

But there's hope! There is always hope. When you don't have strength, simply plead the Blood of Jesus. Plead the Blood over your life. Over your situation. Over your circumstance. This should be your first and last resort. It is the greatest power given to us by our Heavenly Father! Learn how to harness it effectively and be certain your inner circle knows how to as well.

Above all else, guard your heart, for everything you do flows from it (Proverbs 4:23 NIV).

It is wise to protect your peace and guard your

heart. The scriptures tell us this, but scriptures also tell us *not* to fear. If you find *protection of self* seeping over into *distrust of most*, then your protection tactics have gotten out of balance. It is time for re-alignment!

The good news is nothing lasts forever. This means your pain is undoubtedly temporary. You should also know your pain is purposeful. Romans 8:28 tells us, "And we know that in all things God works for the good of those who love him, who have been called according to his purpose."

I certainly found purpose in my pain. I can still hear how the Holy Spirit spoke to me about writing a book about my testimony during my miscarriages. My pain was so heavy, and I was in such great grief, I didn't see how I could do it. But I mustered up the strength to start journaling. I journaled in an old notebook. And I second-guessed the entire time. And God still took those journal entries written by *frightened me* to spread hope. Those *scaredy-cat* journal entries were the foundation for the book I would eventually write after I began birthing my babies. My pain not only birthed a book, but it birthed a ministry – Fertility Hope! Fertility Hope started with testimonies on social media when I was six months pregnant with my firstborn, Justice. Through Fertility Hope, I have hosted a brunch and a conference. Thank God for the help of friends! I have preached Fertility Hope in The Bahamas. I have shared the testimony of Fertility Hope on a few stages and across a few digital platforms. Fertility Hope has been featured on a news broadcast and in magazines. Fertility Hope has been preached on a secular panel alongside a popular reality TV star! As my husband and I shout, ONLY BELIEVE whenever God prompts! My heart has grieved alongside many who have lost children and celebrated alongside many who have seen God fulfill promises, for they now hold live babies in their hands. Fertility Hope even brought about the title of this book – as I was prophesied over at a fertility conference by a stranger who called me *Broken Leader*.

Yes, there is purpose in your pain, my friend. If you are currently experiencing a season of hardship, know this: *Trouble Don't Last Always!*[2] Also, don't attempt to analyze *it* while you're in *it*. It is a waste of time. Instead, *feel*. Instead, *grieve*. Know these processes are human and necessary. Retrain your mind to understand these are not dirty words. Give way to your emotions. Give way to what you feel. Take time to grieve. Catharsis is good. Also, whatever simple pleasantries you may indulge while undergoing your difficult season, do so if they allow you to cope well. Also know, it is okay to step away from supporting others (*outside your home*) while healing. And, it is okay to ask for help with some of your normal *at-home* responsibilities while you cope. Counseling is an awesome tool! Seek it. Beyond the advisement of your Spiritual leader(s), seek counseling from a licensed professional. While there is Spiritual work to be done, there is practical work to be done in tandem.

Go on walks. Exercise. Go to the gym. Sing in the shower. Listen to music. Phone a friend. Go to church – *even if remotely*. Be creative. Color. Draw. Paint. Write. Put puzzles together. Go to events – especially the free ones! Laugh. Truly laugh out loud! Talk to a child you love every once and a while. Try new things. Eat good food. Go to the movies. Go to the library. *Actually*, check out a hardcopy book. Go to the park. Stop and smell the roses! Limit trash intake. Take social media breaks. Ignore the phone call. Do something mindless every now and again. Do chores. Sweep. Vacuum. Wash the dishes (*by hand*). Load the dishwasher. Fold laundry. Start a garden. Water the grass. Play board games. If you're a parent, indulge in childlike silliness *with your kids*. If you're not, volunteer and do this with underserved children. Travel. Go on staycations. Cry on somebody's bosom. Be on the prayer call. Don't be on the prayer call. Breathe ... Be kind ... to yourself. *Just be.*

Whew! You can do this! Allow the leader within to be nourished. Allow the leader within to be cultivated. Allow the leader within to thrive. Allow the leader within to be herself. And don't apologize! Stop excusing your existence. You belong in the world. God set it to be so before He placed you in your mother's womb.

For you created my inmost being; you knit me together in my mother's womb. I praise you because I am fearfully and wonderfully made; your works are wonderful, I know that full well. My frame was not hidden from you when I was made in the secret place, when I was woven together in the depths of the earth. Your eyes saw my unformed body; all the days ordained for me were written in your book before one of them came to be. (Psalm 139: 13-16 NIV)

Cracked identity no more! Let the potter put you back together again. Stop second-guessing. You were born to lead, and you were made a leader. Consecrate yourself and commit yourself to prayer. Ask God to be your guide. Ask God to help you become Spirit-led and put down leading by the flesh. It's time to be serious about who God says you are! No more games. Just as easy as it was for you to adopt the lies the adversary said about your identity, easily decide to put them down today. Reject and rebuke all evil from coming anywhere near you by the Blood of the Lamb slain for our sins' sake. Thank God for the hedge of protection placed around you every day. Relinquish control and be healed. Resist going from broken to *bitter.* Embrace the broken pieces of your heart and *believe* God has your best interest in His heart always!

Pray This:

Our Father who art in heaven, hallowed be Your name. Your kingdom come, your will be done, on earth as it is in heaven. Give us this day our daily bread, and forgive us our debts, as we have forgiven our debtors. And lead us not into temptation, but deliver us from evil. For thine is the Kingdom and the power and the Glory. Forever. Amen. (Matthew 6:9-13; Luke 11:2-4)

God is with you. Everything will be alright. Be restored in Jesus' Name!

WELL, LOOK AT YOU! YOU HAVE FINISHED STEP THREE! MEET ME IN THE MIRROR CLEANING STUDY GUIDE FOR THE THIRD EXERCISE. THERE IS MUCH GOOD WORK FOR US TO DO!

STEP FOUR:

Broken Hope – The Remedy for Your Kryptonite

Devotional

Romans 8.7-9 NRSV -

For this reason the mind that is set on the flesh is hostile to God; it does not submit to God's law - indeed it cannot, and those who are in the flesh cannot please God. But you are not in the flesh; you are in the Spirit, since the Spirit of God dwells in you. Anyone who does not have the Spirit of Christ does not belong to him.

This scripture may feel like a heavy declaration, so allow me to make it bite-sized. We have the free will to act of our own volition (*flesh*), but it is better to listen for and follow God's Holy Spirit. When you follow as *Spirit* leads, life can be full of beautiful surprises. If you instead follow the flesh, you may just find yourself leading from the *break*. The break which separated you from *hope*. In extreme settings, it becomes a form of self-sabotage – kryptonite to your superpower.

In 2019, I took my daughter to the Lilly Frilly Enchanted Experience - a wonderful event for mothers and daughters. It was a grand affair! Learning about it last minute, I questioned if we should go. I also wondered if it mattered because Broughton was so young. It was a month before her third birthday, and I was very pregnant! Thankfully, after a vivid dream, confirming the Lord's tug in my spirit, I felt good about trying this *new thing*. Our experience is one of the greatest memories I have shared with my daughter during her early years. In all her beauty, brightness, and curiosity, it brought me such joy to watch her eyes glimmer at the sights!

Courtney Adeleye, the beauty mogul multimillionaire businesswoman and philanthropist, hosted this delightful affair. It was in celebration of the launch of her young daughter's business, Lilly Frilly. Lilly Frilly toured its Enchanted Experience across several cities in the US. The cost of admission was to purchase your daughter a dress from the Lilly Frilly collection - offering beautiful yet affordable options. I didn't know what to expect, but we were happy to go and see.

The Atlanta Edition granted access to a wonderful afternoon at the beautiful Biltmore Hotel. Multiple courses served by wait staff and tables featuring dessert and snack bars lined the walls. There were also elaborate photo booths, face painting, henna stations, and even tiaras customed by hand on-site with live flowers and toy jewels, paired with scepters. Just glorious! The mothers and daughters were seated in chivari chairs in our own separate sections. The food was immaculate! The mothers were served a grilled fillet of beef with a cabernet demi sauce and sautéed shrimp with lemon-chive butter over parmesan mashed potatoes and roasted vegetables for the main course while our daughters enjoyed a kid-friendly dish of chicken fingers, mac and cheese, and fruit. There was dancing and even slime! I was amazed! There was no stone unturned, and everything served was of quality. I imagine this says a lot about Mrs. Adeleye's heart. She even took the time to take photographs with those who were willing to wait in line. We were sure to be *two* in the number.

    Our family, not going out as much at the time, decided to make it a day in the city. So, following, we met up with Jerrell and Justice and decided to head over to Atlantic Station for early dinner and browsing merchandise. Dinner did not turn out for the best as our meal suffered from a few issues at one of our old favorite spots, and we were all tired from the long day. Anxious to leave after feeling like we were being held hostage while waiting on our bill, I went to the restroom and asked Jerrell to keep the children with him. Thinking we agreed to meet out front, I quickly relieved myself and waddled out the door expecting to see the rest of my family there.

    I looked in the lobby of the restaurant. I looked outside. I gazed across the street. I walked back inside the restaurant – thinking maybe they were in the restroom. I walked back outside after some time. After several minutes, I eventually became very tired and decided to rest on a bench, thinking, surely, they would eventually cross my path. I'm sure you're thinking, "Where was your cell phone?" Well, it was dead. Also, Jerrell's phone was dying. *Bad. I know.* At first, it was okay because I knew they would find me, but then it felt like 30 minutes had passed, and I became very anxious. Though I was in pain and extremely fatigued, I walked down to the underground parking deck to attempt to find our vehicle. Those who know me know this was a big mistake. My weakness is my visual-spatial ability. I became extremely hot, my feet were hurting, and the rest of my body was aching badly. I was concerned I might pass out in the deck, and no one would find me as I struggled to find the truck.

My efforts were unsuccessful. My family was still nowhere to be found. So, I fought with all my might to return to the above-ground bench outside the restaurant. I sat there some more, and I was near tears as the sun was setting. I began to fear something bad had happened to my beloved. Next, I had to think of a non-threatening approach to ask a stranger to allow me to use a cell phone. Thankfully, a nice lady with her daughters obliged. I was able to phone Jerrell and reunite with my family once again. Jerrell had made his way back to the car and charged his phone by this time. I'm unsure how long we were separated – estimation of numbers is also not one of my strengths. I do know it was long enough for me to feel abandoned. For clarity, my husband is one of the most devoted and loyal to those he loves (*me – especially*) people I know, so it is not in his nature to leave me anywhere. But that didn't stop the fear and the devil from having their hands on working to sabotage the beautiful day I had up until that point. Following, I only wanted to go home and lay in bed. Even in the midst of my fear, I could feel the presence of God. I *knew* God was with me. God was whispering to me and prompting me to return to sit back on that bench. That bench was in a high-traffic area. If something were to happen to me, more people would be likely to witness it, and if my husband were to return to the restaurant, I would be in his line of sight.

For the record, just as I was searching for Jerrell and the kids, they were searching for me. They were even yelling my name out. I just couldn't hear them. It seemed we kept going to opposite positions when one of us should have probably remained in one location longer, so we might meet again sooner. Have you ever felt your hope was so broken you feared your flesh was positioning you away from God's Spirit? Yeah. I know. It can happen, but there's a cure! Your remedy is yield to the Spirit of

God which dwells within. Establish before hell you belong to God. Your hope shall be repaired again. Simply reach beyond the break!

A Peek through My Window

I enjoyed my relationship with my father very much when I was young. He was brilliant, very charismatic, a lot of fun and the life of the party. Unfortunately, he developed addictions which drew him away from our family and led to my parents' eventual divorce. Despite the many years passed since my father's departure from my childhood home, I recognize my issues with abandonment have origins here. Wanting to believe the best in everyone, and particularly my father, I had very high hopes when he would leave our home for periods of time. I hoped for his return and hoped he would return sober and never leave again.

To my dismay, I vividly remember just before my father left for good, how prompted by my young mother – fighting to keep herself and her family together, seventh grade-me said to my dad, "It's better for you to be gone all the time than to be in and out." I said these words with the hope in my heart my father would take this ultimatum and choose us! It was the right thing to do. I wanted him to stay with his family. My young mind clearly did not understand the disease of addiction just yet. I had not yet learned the pain of the fact: *addiction has no family*.

It took some time and some therapy, but I have finally realized I blamed myself for my mother, brother, and I never having him ever again. I blamed myself so much until I would nearly do anything to get people to stay in my life. As a youth, I literally had kids steal from me, and I knew it, but I pretended I didn't to salvage the relationships. I've had people call me out my name, and I laugh it off because I wanted to be nice. I wanted to be able to make the claim I wasn't responsible for pushing them away. I have been loyal to a fault to individuals who I probably was only meant to *pass by* on my journey. Perhaps extend a helping hand to someone hurting, but instead of keeping my path, I've stopped and diverted to their own. I have allowed people to utterly mistreat me without correction and blame it on being a good Christian when this is not true. The truth is, I have been afraid of being abandoned *again*.

If you've journeyed with God for any length of time, you probably guessed how God handled this fear. Yep, that's right! I've been abandoned (*called to part ways*) time and time again. I've been left behind in friendship. I've been left behind in business. I pride myself in maintaining my good character, despite how I've been wronged. Not simply due to my integrity alone, as *I'd like to believe*, but more-so to not give the one who leaves anything on me.

At this stage of my life, the most valuable state of being to me is *at peace*. I will pay any amount of money for it, and I will go to the depths of the earth to find it. Historically, I won't argue with individuals even when they have the facts wrong, when it's time for them to leave me. Now, the upside is God has provided opportunities for those who've wronged me in the past to either reconcile the wrong or bless me in the future. This might be indirect at times. But God always proves Himself as my vindicator! Let me clarify; I am no fool. I know just as surely as I have felt wronged, there must be others who have felt wronged and even abandoned by me, and I may not be aware. But the good news is, God can heal us all.

A byproduct of my struggle with abandonment is comparison. Comparison, not in the sense of wanting the things others have. Thankfully, I have been raised to be content with my blessings. Instead, comparison has punished me through feelings of inadequacy. I have felt as though people should see my gifts and talents, but I fear instead, they see me in a diminished way or as inadequate. As though something about me goes *unseen*, and I will be falsely mislabeled as *not up to par*. It is a strange occurrence and almost difficult to describe. It is also very new for me to identify this. What is immediately apparent is yet another sneaky attack by the adversary to fight me for my gift. My *voice* is my gift. Whether I wield it through my mouth or my pen, the power of words is the weapon God has given me to utilize on earth for the Kingdom's advancement.

Understand, the same way the enemy fights me for my voice, he has done this to my bloodline for generations. As the songwriter, Jonathan McReynolds, says, "He has me going in cycles." *Cycles.* There is evidence of this linearly and laterally. April D. Wesley discusses this phenomenon in her book, *Queenship Restored: The Reconciliation of the Alpha Woman*. She testifies one doesn't have to look far to understand how the enemy will attack your life. She proposes you will see how the enemy repeatedly tries the same tactics within a family tree if you simply look back. She also stresses the importance of a family sharing what it has overcome with younger generations vs. keeping secrets. My favorite quote during her discussion around this at her book signing was, "The devil is lame. He uses the same old tricks."

Cycles no more! Cry out to God. God can heal you and repair your hope. God knows exactly where and when the break occurred. God's bonding agent is far better than any superglue out there! God knows how to remedy the Kryptonite pulling on your superpower in this very moment. Yes, the flesh is hostile to God because *it wants what it wants*. Your flesh carries the anger and pain of your past circumstances. Choose, instead of the flesh, to be led by God's Spirit. As God's own, God's Spirit will rightfully take you to God's chosen destiny for your life. Be free! Feel abandoned no more. Be bold. No need to compare yourself to His other creations. You were fearfully and wonderfully made! God has broken the chains. You no longer are bound to participate in the devil's cycle. The buck stops here. Today is a new day! Choose to serve God wholeheartedly. *The leader within is just about to break forth!*

Pray This:

Dear Heavenly Father:

Thank You for repairing my broken hope. Thank You for revealing the remedy for the kryptonite that has attempted to break my superpower. Thank You for showing me this new day! I am ready to relinquish the pain of my past completely over to You. I am ready to be healed in Jesus' Name! Thank You for never giving up on me. Thank You for never turning Your back on me. Thank You for never abandoning me. I love You! In Jesus' name, I pray. Amen.

HEAD ON OVER TO THE MIRROR CLEANING STUDY GUIDE TO COMPLETE EXERCISE FOUR. YOU ARE YET ANOTHER STEP CLOSER TO YOUR BREAKTHROUGH!

STEP FIVE:

Brokenness – See the Label to Remove the Label

Devotional

Romans 8.10-11 NRSV –

But if Christ is in you, though the body is dead because of sin, the Spirit is life because of righteousness. If the Spirit of him who raised Jesus from the dead dwells in you, he who raised Christ from the dead will give life to your mortal bodies also through his Spirit that dwells in you.

Christ's ascension from the grave gave way for the Spirit to dwell within. *Spirit* is life. Our bodies should be dead to sin. But we will forever navigate the tug of war between *Spirit* and flesh while here on earth. In the same way we see flesh and know the reality of its limitations, we must also see the label, *brokenness*. For after we see the label and acknowledge it, we can harness power to remove it. Once we begin to operate in *Spirit*, we will operate from our places of restoration. There within, God dwells.

This past weekend we celebrated Pentecost inside our home. Pentecost is believed to be the start of the Christian church and often marks the coming down of the *fire* of the Holy Spirit (see Acts 2). In the middle of a global pandemic: Covid-19 and another age-old virus, racist police brutality. It is a different time. Different from anything my generation has ever experienced before. American citizens and others from various countries worldwide have taken it to the streets to decry the horrific injustices devaluing Black lives. This past weekend was also the 99th anniversary of the Tulsa Massacre, where Black Wall Street was looted and burned to the ground by racist White residents. *Fire*. Triggered by a Black man being falsely accused and with concerns, an angry mob would lynch him, the community showed up in his defense. Under unfair systems, several African Americans were imprisoned, and reports believe as many as 300 were killed. 1,256 homes were *burned* down and destroyed. Additional structures like churches, schools, businesses, a library, and hospitals were obliterated. Reports emphasize no government on any level aided the African Americans of Tulsa in restructuring. In fact, the government was said to impede the rebuilding efforts. The Red Cross is the agency documented to have helped the newly homeless citizens. The massacre was also labeled the *Tulsa Race Riot*, seemingly obstructing the residents' ability to make insurance claims. Damage caused by riots is deemed ineligible for insurance funds.[3]

    This dreadful massacre has a lot in common with today. If only centuries ago, America could have seen the label, *brokenness*, we might have removed this label long ago. Instead, we continue to fight a battle which legislation cannot fix because this is a matter of *heart change*.[4] Until the evil seeds of racism are taken out by their ugly roots, the snake attached to the vine planted by the forefathers of this country will continue to bloom, generation after generation.

Thankfully, the brokenness you feel inside personally only requires *one* heart shift, your own. As the Spirit of God dwells in your body, you will live. Decide today to let God's Spirit rule and tell your flesh to submit to God's authority.

A Peek through My Window

Fire. My mother has a lot of it. Married young, and though things didn't work according to plan, she somehow persevered to see my brother and me through healthy childhoods and raised us to operate independently as adults. We were equipped to not only survive but thrive within this society. And like most, she made mistakes, but she has never allowed any setback to keep her from reaching the finish line for any goal she has in life! Tenacity was necessary for my mother to do what life has obligated. Having to drop out of undergrad to take care of us did not stop her from returning and later matriculating to earning her Doctor of Education years later.

Yes, I highly regard my mother and all she sacrificed so her children might have. I am also a witness to what life has robbed from her. I naturally inherited a great bit of her personality, *for better or for worse*. Being seen as overbearing as a young undergraduate, I cringed anytime anyone would refer to me as bossy. It was evident I would need to learn how to better harness my gifts. It would require the balance of knowing when and *when not* to utilize specific aspects of my leadership abilities accordingly. Now, it is not lost on me that men never seem to have this problem, but it is not my present goal to dig into gender role disparities. Instead, let's talk about the birth of this leader.

As a mother, I now completely understand who my mother is and how she operates far more than before having my own children. But the reality is I was very afraid of my mother for many years. I did not always feel comfortable sharing my authentic thoughts with her or my plans. She was forceful and forthright in her efforts to guide me on the right path, but I was looking for *the nurturer.* The nurturer was forced to be strong because of our dismantled *traditional* family unit. My greatest fear was when people would call me bossy in a negative way, I was taking on negative aspects of my mother's character. This was rooted in childhood fears I refused to name for a long time. *Brokenness*. As God began to cultivate me more, I learned being a boss is a part of the leader's nature and is not a negative trait. I also learned approach is everything. There's a reason the old adage says, "you can catch more flies with honey than with vinegar." My mother has told me this many times.

As I worked hard to find how to present my true self to those around me, sometimes I fumbled. After all, I am an externalizer. I often process my thoughts aloud and in conversation. I get very excited and inspired easily when a fresh idea drops in my spirit. I often like to share what I am thinking spontaneously. Other times, I am an over-analyzer and rehearse how I'd like to speak about a difficult topic so much, fear takes over, and I completely bomb. Through many trial runs with close friends and loved ones, I've learned it is not always best to present your raw ideas and emotions to the world. This is something reserved for one or two who are very close to you and have known you long enough to understand how you operate without easily taking offense. The fact is, as discussed in a previous chapter, many people view situations through the lens of their pain. If you are a talker (*as am I*), your spontaneous words and thoughts, no matter how well-meaning, may be misconstrued and weaponized by the enemy even when you are unaware, though it is not your intention. Another remedy for this is to take a moment to *pause and reflect* on what you want to say and self-edit before releasing. This can be helpful. Frankly, as a wordsmith, it's high time I master this ability in my conversations, just as well as in written accounts.

When you forsake these things, relationships become strained, and it's easy to begin walking on eggshells with others – even those you love. I have historically felt moments between my mom and me where it seemed we were both holding our breath between statements in efforts not to offend each other (*or set the other off*) when emotions are high. Whew! This can be exhausting, but successful gains can be achieved over time if both parties are willing to put in the work. It's also worth it!

Are you ready to see the label so you can remove it? Let's face it, if the same things have triggered you for more than a decade, it is clear those issues remain unresolved. And yes, I am very familiar with knowing some pain you will carry with you for a lifetime, but I can also attest if you commit to coping well, you will become more at peace and less bothered by external factors going forward. Are you willing? The leader inside you depends on you to break forth.

Pray This:

Dear Heavenly Father:

Thank You for helping me see my brokenness. Having labeled myself as such is nothing to be ashamed of and, most importantly, not to be swept under the rug. I know You are a healer, and I know You can heal this brokenness inside. I know You possess the power to remove this label from me. Father, I ask that you please do so today. Father, please help me. I am unable to do this on my own. With You and You alone, I can. Please direct my path. In Jesus' Name, I pray. Amen.

HEAD ON OVER TO THE MIRROR CLEANING STUDY GUIDE AND COMPLETE EXERCISE FIVE. YOU'VE GOT THIS!

STEP SIX:
Gracefully Broken – Realizing God Uses It All

Devotional

Romans 8.12-14 NRSV –

So then, brothers and sisters, we are debtors, not to the flesh, to live according to the flesh—for if you live according to the flesh, you will die, but if by the Spirit you put to death the deeds of the body, you will live. For all who are led by the Spirit of God are children of God.

It can feel awkward yielding to The Spirit while denying the flesh. Simply, because God blessed us to walk in these earthly vessels, holding our hearts, minds, organs and tissues. How do you know when to operate with your practical wisdom if fearing it's yet another adversarial trap? How do you know when to wait for further instruction from God's Holy Spirit versus moving on whatever makes the most practical sense in the moment? The answer is govern yourself by God's Holy Spirit at all times. When practical wisdom is chosen for the Believer, it will always line up with what God has previously revealed in Spirt (*which aligns with Bible*). Believers often think on struggles between flesh versus The Spirit of God within. But what happens when The Spirit of God within is at battle with *fleshy* others around you?

After leaving the first job I took to move to Atlanta, I struggled for a bit. I cried alone in my apartment. I tried to seek God and would fall asleep as one of my friends challenged me to lay prostrate before Him. I was taking advice from everyone. I attended job fair after job fair and more job fairs. I was trying my best to get any *adult* job I could find to pay my bills to get me over the hump. This was exhausting.

Finally, I went to another job fair housed at a megachurch. This church was huge. I am saying this to say, I believe God put me in this physically challenging situation so I might grow tired enough. Tired enough to listen. Tired enough to remember what brought me here in the first place and tired enough to pursue purpose! I could not afford to play the numbers game at this job fair. I decided to instead use the map I was provided upon entry to only search for opportunities at nonprofit organizations. You see, when I was called to Atlanta from my hometown, it went a little something like this: I was sitting in an annual conference service of the AME church listening to the sermon. While the preacher was preaching, I was resting in the presence of The Holy Spirit. Specifically, I was no longer listening to the sermon. I was listening to *THE SPIRIT!* God began to download a Rhema word into my belly. God said to me, "Valencya, you're going to move to Atlanta. You're going to move to Atlanta to start a nonprofit organization!" As my spirit leaped for joy, I had no idea what was *up the road ahead of me*. This is why I decided only to visit the NPOs at the fair. I remember locating *just one*.

When I arrived in the room where the table was located, I was saddened to learn they weren't hiring but were searching for AmeriCorps volunteers to tutor young children in K-12 schools instead. In undergrad, I was a mentor, and I tutored. And, I've always loved children. But frankly, I felt I'd done enough volunteering. It was time for me to bring home the bacon! When my charm couldn't appeal to the representatives for the long-term position - *which was unavailable*, I reluctantly took the AmeriCorps application and completed the interest form. My interest piqued a little when I learned a stipend and an education award were involved, which could be applied retroactively. I then thought to myself, why not give it a shot? You like kids, and the stipend does provide some money. So, go for it and figure out the rest later.

At that age, I believed in running my life's decisions past quite a few people. As I started to take the *Gallup poll* on what should be next for my journey, the majority were opposed. I can still hear my grandmother's voice, albeit well-meaning, "How are you going to pay your bills? How will you pay your car note?" I cringed. Back then, I was known for leaping and then figuring things out later. Additionally, I felt like God confirmed it was the right move, but my need to *feel* approval from others at the time *made me feel* bad. Thankfully, even when I was younger, even if I felt confused, I would dive right in if I felt The Lord brought me to it! So off I went! Would you know, in this program, I was blessed and favored? Once accepted, I got wind of interviews for a special opportunity to serve a local university. So, I expressed my interest. Thankfully, I did because I was told, "Oh, we didn't think you would like such an opportunity." With a background as a Residence Assistant while in undergrad, I was accustomed to working with students at the collegiate level. Would you know I was the absolute last person interviewed, and I was selected for the position?

I did not know this position came with on-campus housing (*no more rent!*), a meal plan (*free food!*), travel opportunities, and attending an array of cultural events. I was also provided an inside look at many non-profit organizations and schools within the metro Atlanta area. This was most certainly one of the greatest experiences of my young adult life! I liked it so much I was hoping to get hired for a more permanent position, but there were none. Thankfully, you can serve two consecutive terms as an AmeriCorps volunteer, and they were happy to have me. But I didn't take this second term lightly. Instead, I decided to research and select which local graduate program I would attend following, met with professors to ask what things were necessary for me to excel as an applicant, and pursued them! Even when I thought, "There's no way I'm doing that. That's too much work!" But I accomplished it all. The grace of God literally got me through them all.

This is how it can be when you allow yourself to be broken in God's grace. Becoming *gracefully broken*. I was truly perplexed about how my path didn't go as planned near the end of undergrad. I found myself frustrated at many bends and turns in the road. Thankfully, I didn't let go. This doesn't mean I didn't consider it – as I struggled with the enemy's taunts at my lowest points. By God's grace through my brokenness, I prevailed. I won't say, *in spite of*. Because God uses everything, I will say *because of*. Full disclosure, as this may help someone, I considered suicide once. I found out about the GRE being required for grad school last minute and took the test without any form of preparation. This was the first standardized test I'd received to provide a score on the screen immediately after. It may have also been my first computerized test.

Lo and behold I did not pass.

Following, I was driving my vehicle over a bridge from one of the islands *off* Charleston, South Carolina. I distinctly recall a rushed voice saying, "You should drive into the water now because your life is over." The voice was trying to convince me the failed test would keep me from graduate school and keep me from succeeding in life. I am certain this was the adversary! For a split second, I considered it, I may have even steered the car in the direction of the water, but just as soon as the thought came, with tears in my eyes, somehow, I put it away and kept driving on the road. I remember crying so hard until my vision was obstructed, but I made it safely to my dorm. *That was God*!

If you are leading with your own flesh instead of God's spirit, it's far easier to fall victim. Victim to advice of others also leading by flesh and Satan, the enemy. Guard your heart and follow God's Spirit over *all* flesh at all times. Discern God's voice and direction through prayer. Whatever practical wisdom you have attained is by God's grace. If you find yourself in a confused state while discerning what's next, continue working on the last *right* thing you are confident God told you to do. And if you are overtaken by worry or making fearful decisions, know this – God will never cause you to make rushed decisions. That is *not ever* God. Yes, there are things which must be completed quickly – during which you may receive a call to move swiftly by the Holy Spirit. This is different from hapazard rushing. Yes, you might be scared to try new things. After all, you are only human. But if you find yourself shrinking, think again. Stretch to where God is calling you to go. Find biblical accounts which reveal God's promises. Look back over God's proven track record in your own life. Govern yourself accordingly.

You have to turn the light on so you can see.

– Justice Thompson (my 7-year-old)

A Peek through My Window

I moved to Atlanta at 23 years young from my hometown, Columbia, SC. I was eager to get to this city – which was the land of opportunity for many African Americans at the time. Determined, with my Bachelor of Science in Psychology degree in hand, I struggled to be taken seriously with each phone call placed. I reached out to my network, harnessing any help I could to get a job. Finally, a friend said, "take any job to move to the city; once you move, you can take your time to look for something in line with your goals." Have you ever gone somewhere and forgot why you went? It's like walking from one room to another in your home. Then your mind goes blank in seconds. This is very frustrating! The same is when God positions you somewhere with instructions to remain for a brief season. Yet, you become sucked into the culture when you were supposed to be passing through. *Yep, very frustrating.* The good news is God, through Jesus Christ, His son, is our redeemer. And God redeems time. It reminds me of a scripture reference from the book of Ruth where we see an exchange between Boaz and another relative who was closer in kinship to Naomi's deceased husband. See Boaz as *God*. Ruth 4:4b – 6 NRSV says:

> "If you will redeem it, redeem it; but if you will not, tell me, so that I may know; for there is no one prior to you to redeem it, and I come after you." So he said, "I will redeem it. Then Boaz said, "The day you acquire the field from the hand of

> *Naomi, you are also acquiring Ruth the Moabite, the widow of the dead man, to maintain the dead man's name on his inheritance." At this, the next-of-kin said, "I cannot redeem it for myself without damaging my own inheritance. Take my right of redemption yourself, for I cannot redeem it."*

Notice how the next of kin does not want to take on the added responsibility of marrying Ruth while he has shown up to acquire Naomi's land. Harper Collins Biblical commentary indicates Boaz readily "accepts the double obligation of acquiring the land and Ruth" and "Boaz's loyalty to family emerges strongly."[5] See God as stepping up to the plate ready to take full responsibility for your life. Every problem. Every situation. Every circumstance. Give it over today.

The job which *moved* me to *da A* was with a major retailer. A friend coached me on negotiating my salary, but I cowered when the interviewers chuckled at my request. I was lowballed into a lower pay tier. To top it off, I was manager and peer simultaneously (*yep – a set-up*) to a group of older women. I'm talking I was 23, and those I supervised were managers ranging mid/late 40s to 60s. Likely, the only advantage I had was a college degree and the store manager seeking a new ally. Our leader was also young. Though I was unsure of her exact age, I could tell, and she told me never reveal mine. It was no use. Even now nearly 40, I still wear my baby face. First, the store leader sent me to another store for some training. Second, I was trained by one of the ladies who would soon report to me. I was told to tell her leadership was still unsure of my role. This felt wrong. I felt out of place, and it showed. Sometimes the team shared information with me because it was required. Other times I was ignored. The remaining times I was bullied and mocked.

I learned a lot about the *big city* from my welcome committee. And every day, I felt as though every one of my weaknesses were on display. I was overly anxious. I cried in corners. I could barely sleep at night. I lost so much weight until my grandmother said, "They must have you running all around that store!" But I knew better. *I was stressed*. The perfect ingredients for my feelings of abandonment to resurface. This time I feared God abandoned me.

Well-intentioned, I attempted to meet with friends to launch our non-profit during downtime, but our efforts soon waned and I was learning. *I was learning*. As a visionary, I was expected to lead our efforts, and I was expected to invest the most time. I was 20-something. I had no clue. I also learned how exhaustion due to a lack of boundaries leaves little energy to build. I was learning how being valued - even at work matters to me. This left a little time to do a little research here and there, and with little effort, I hoped things would take off miraculously. Not to mention my husband was my then-boyfriend and our relationship also required *time*. All at once, I was learning many rules for a well-balanced life.

Feeling abandoned. Where does this feeling come from? When you latch onto God's vision, remember God shares portions according to His plan and desires. As a creative or any imaginative person, it is really easy to play out *how you think* God is going to do it. But if you've walked with Him for any length of time, you know it's never *quite that way*. Yes, our God is amazing, God is miraculous, and He's always up to something! And when you experience those *between moments* (pain and uncertainty), it's so easy to think God has forgotten you or you've been left behind. Remember, this is not so. God, The Redeemer, is always with you. God is with you now. *God knew you would have this moment. God also knew when it would be!* Trust Him. Have you ever felt like a fish out of water? Well, that's how I felt about this job. I became so bogged down in one of the rare occasions of not being praised for my work and berated by my supervisor while unaccepted by peers; I nearly missed the purpose of this *transitional* position. The position was to serve as my vehicle just to allow me to reach my destination. Somehow, I became sidetracked and tried to treat my vehicle as *home*. Big mistake. Let's break this down. If you struggle with seeking the approval of others, you can waste time trying to prove yourself in areas God never intended. Then you can miss the mark of what you've been called to do in the present season and become completely derailed. Dangerous territory, but the good news is God allows us to be gracefully broken, and God can most certainly use it all! If this applies to your current situation, fret not. Reach out and grab God's hand – just simply ask God to help you refocus on your calling. You can do it! *Believe today*.

    Feeling delayed and confused? Don't worry; this often means you're beginning God's process. What process? Now you're asking the right question! But the answer you seek may only be provided by the Heavenly Father. Go ahead, *ask*. Be prepared to write it down when you hear back.

    I stayed in that temporary location far longer than I should have. Just like someone in the median on a busy highway afraid to pull into a driving lane. I kept trying to make it work until I began seeing evidence of the Holy Spirit pushing me out. Yep. Pushed out. All sorts of craziness began happening on the job. It was as though God was saying, "If you are too afraid to leave when I've called you, I'm going to make you completely uncomfortable until you get the point." I remember the week of my birthday – which I'm very serious about celebrating – I was called to close and was left without other management (*who were paid much higher to be there*) on several occasions. All sorts of mayhem went on. Lost store keys – which I was nearly hyperventilating to find. A customer was hit by a car in the parking lot. A baby leaped out a buggy before my eyes and hit her head on the floor. Employees were non-compliant late at night when it was past time to go home, etc. *It was absolutely bananas*! And, I was like, "*Okay God, I get it! I'm outta here*!" I put in my two weeks' notice the next morning. My supervisor was so angry she didn't allow me to complete my two weeks. I learned another life rule. Stack your paper when you're planning to leave a job in case there is retaliation! And let's be honest, you have no clue how long you will have to wait to find your next gig. Stay the course. Be faithful to the voice of God. *He will direct Your path.*

All in all, my flesh was on the warpath to prove I could do something I wasn't called to do. It was waging war against the flesh of others when I should have remained connected enough to tap into God's Spirit and determine a viable course of action for *the transitional place*. Now, there are many times when God will call you to a temporary location without providing a schedule. However, remain connected to *The Source*; you will be better able to *ready yourself for walking* God's path as the Holy Spirit leads.

Whenever you are going through a tough season, God will send an ally in some form to remind you of His presence and guide you towards the light at the end of the tunnel. *Sounds just like The Redeemer, doesn't it?* I'm reminded of two such allies even now. When I was in this position, God sent me a handful of people who would check on me inside the store. Two were Ms. Mattie and Ms. Roberta. Two beautiful seniors who loved to fold clothes side by side. Ms. Mattie and Ms. Roberta took delight when I ran a shift because I did not separate them, as other managers might. When my two found out

I was leaving, they said they wanted to take me out for a surprise. They guided me down the interstate as I drove the three of us to a small town off I-20 called Social Circle. To my surprise, they took me to a beautiful tearoom. We were able to brunch and have tea as they loved on me. It was truly a blessed time! A spotlight in my dark moment. Know this, *you have been gracefully broken, indeed.* God knows, and God will use it all.

Pray This:

Dear Heavenly Father:

Thank You for grace in brokenness. I admit as a human, it is not fun to be broken, nor does it sound attractive to pursue. Thank You for the reminder, You know what I don't, and You think at a different level than I. Thank You for not leaving me behind in my ignorance. I am forever grateful for Your love and for how You fight for me. Thank You for being My Redeemer, and thank You for redeeming my time. In Jesus' Name, I pray. Amen.

LOOK AT THE MOMENTUM YOU ARE MAKING! I AM SUPER PROUD OF YOU! JUMP ON OVER TO THE MIRROR CLEANING STUDY GUIDE AND LET'S GET TO WORK ON EXERCISE SIX. DESTINY AWAITS.

STEP SEVEN:

Beyond Repair - Can I Be Put Back Together Again?

Devotional

Romans 8.15-17 NRSV –

For you did not receive a spirit of slavery to fall back into fear, but you have received a spirit of adoption. When we cry, "Abba! Father!" it is that very Spirit bearing witness with our spirit that we are children of God, and if children, then heirs, heirs of God and joint heirs with Christ - if, in fact, we suffer with him so that we may also be glorified with him.

Beyond Repair.

Agent: "Yes, Ma'am. We're going to go ahead and total it out."

Valencya: "But wait, it was a simple fender bender!"

Agent: "Yeah, that's true, but the Blue Book value is so low it is beyond repair." "So, we'll issue you a check in the amount of $2,934.57."

Valencya: "Oh yeah, and what kind of car am I supposed to buy with that?" "I need to get to work like ASAP."

Agent: "Sorry, Ma'am. Thank you for choosing _____ to service your car insurance needs."

(*Click*)

I've seen my share of accidents. In this life, we're bound to see a few. But nothing makes you feel like you can't win more than going through a struggle season - only to be toppled over by further delays. It's like being hit by a ton of bricks. After which, you toss up your hands, throw your head back and shout, "What's the use?"

I'm here right now to remind you to snap back into it! God is not calling you into position to quit, and God does not want you to be enslaved by fear any longer. Instead, remind yourself, you belong to God, and God is your Heavenly Father. Christ is your redeemer and your brother! This means whatever Christ inherits, so do you. *Good and bad.* But hopefully, you'll see more of the good in this life. Whatever season you are in, never believe the lie your circumstance is beyond repair. And never believe *you* are beyond repair! God is putting you back together as we speak. The process is much better once you relinquish control. Remind yourself, "God is not a man that He should lie..." (Numbers 23:19). What God said, God will do. Stick it out. Don't throw in the towel. Be honest with God about how you feel. He already knows anyway.

A Peek through My Window

I can recall dreaming of having a significant other to love me as early as elementary school. This desire was fueled by my searching for a replacement for the lack of feeling my father's love in tangible ways. Understand, whenever I saw him, he always said he loved me as he does even now, but his absence denied the opportunity to show this love consistently. Though I'm thankful for how my grandparents supported my Mom in caring for my brother and me, something was still missing. An easy fix I found as a young girl was through validation received from boys *liking me*. No matter how fickle friendship from young boys may be, I vied for their attention. It was bizarre because I even entertained the bullies who threatened to beat the entire team up (*me included*) if we lost the kickball game in PE class. Whew!

Like me, I'm sure you're questioning what this specifically has to do with being a broken leader? Well, I asked God the same question. The response: "Everything that gets in the way applies." Yes, my friend, baggage like this adds to our unnecessary stops on the journey. These extra stops literally stop us from leading as we have been called.

By the time I reached high school, I knew I was pretty because I was raised to be self-confident, but I never quite felt good enough to be liked by a decent guy. Frankly, the guys I entertained for a while didn't match. I was tracked in advanced, honors, and AP courses, and they were barely getting by. There were a host of other areas mismatched as well. It was hard for me to believe when I finally encountered a guy who made sense for me to date, who shared a mutual physical attraction and interest in being *boyfriend & girlfriend*. I mean, he was interested in me; wow! After falling for each other, *albeit prematurely*, I planned our entire lives together. When plans failed, I became completely derailed. Following our final break up during the summer of matriculating to my sophomore year in college, I struggled with trying my hand at dating again. All while trying to define myself as a conscious woman, making false starts to learn exactly who she was and establish *who she was* simultaneously. I cared about social justice causes and joined organizations to learn more and effectuate change in my local communities. I cared, and I was looking for someone to care for me. Even then, God was working to grab my attention.

Oh, how I loved God! I always have, but no one taught me how to tame the flesh or what to do with those untimely desires until that point in my life. I struggled to balance it all the best I could. *Faith. Citizenship. Womanhood. Unapologetically Black. Lover of All. Leader.*

Oh, the leader within was being broken in all sorts of ways. I was bothered whenever I witnessed disorganization – whether in a formal meeting or at a friendly gathering. When others were afraid to speak up, I felt compelled to do so. Someone had to. *Right?* Then there were other moments where I thought people had grown tired of hearing my voice. So, I'd shrink. *Just a little*. Here and there. I've missed moments when I've known for certain what to do, but I didn't want to be viewed as *that* person. You know the one. The one that always has an answer, and people roll their eyes before she utters her first syllable. I've struggled between wanting to be liked and saying what's right. According to Dallas Willard, as told by John Ortberg in *Soul Keeping: Caring for the Most Important Part of You*, "Being right is actually a very hard burden to be able to carry gracefully and humbly. That's why nobody likes to sit next to the kid in class who's right all the time. One of the hardest things in the world is to be right and not hurt other people with it."

This brokenness played on me terribly. So much until, when I didn't stumble upon the right guy quick enough *for my liking*, I believed the enemy's false narrative, I was likely destined to become a *Single Soul*. The devil is a liar! What God has for me is for me. And what God has for you is for you.

Yes, I truly did allow the enemy to have his way for a while. My thoughts and my views were skewed, though well-intentioned. As *a misled – serial empathy dater* (yep, I named it), I was dating *nice*, as in being nice to ensure I would never be alone. What I was missing, is God was there the entire time. He never left me. And He has never left you. It is of the utmost importance that you grasp this today! I believe this is one of the greatest tactics the enemy uses against the kingdom of God – *isolation*. Yes, the adversary has always had a goal in mind to get you alone in your thoughts. This way, he can flood you with all sorts of untruths when your guard is down, and you're not wearing your armor as you should be.

There is a reason Ephesians 6:11 commands us to "put on the whole armor of God," this spiritual protective gear is essential in shielding us from the enemy's attacks. And when your guard is down, at least if you have close communion with a few other believers, they can raise a shield on your behalf. A friend in the body can *cover your face* when you feel you no longer have the strength to protect yourself. But if you've weakened to a place where you allow yourself to become isolated, it's easy to be much more vulnerable to the enemy's blows. A broken heart in isolation gives the enemy many advantages. There is no one to remind you of God's truths. There's no one to remind you of God's promises. When you've allowed your inner self to become so clouded by confusion and you are missing what the Holy Spirit is saying, it's easy to fall into a trap set *just for you*.

About that armor. I once had a vision while sleeping. The Holy Spirit actually presented it to me in my early 20's to educate me on the power He'd provided for us, His children, to harness. God showed me a motion picture of myself in a boxing ring. My opponent was Satan. As I saw the devil in the ring across from me, it was clear we were mid-fight. Instead of physically punching him with protected hands in boxing gloves, the Holy Spirit prompted me to recite scripture. And every time God's Holy Word projected from my mouth, the adversary literally became visibly weaker. The devil's physical form, as presented before me, was bending over with every blow. I repeat, I was not punching him with my hands, but I was literally obliterating him as I recited God's Holy Words aloud!

Whenever you find your mind under attack, particularly while being awake in bed, be sure to rebuke the devil and call on the Word of God out loud! It is imperative to rebuke the adversary aloud because, as a minister taught me years ago, the devil cannot hear our thoughts. He does not know them. God is the only omniscient being. On the other hand, and thankfully for our sake, you can whisper a prayer in your heart, never uttering a sound from your lips, and God will hear it. God is watching over, ready, prepared to send 10,000 angels to your defense right now.

Stop falling into the fear trap.

Imagine your natural habitat is the jungle. Every morning you walk outside your dwelling, you walk down a cleared path to collect water. You've followed this same routine all your life, and you know your hunter has set a trap for you approximately 30 feet down the path. The trap never moves. As a matter of fact, it's remained in the same location for years! Yet, for some reason, you're never prepared for it. You allow yourself to become distracted by your own *insignificant* thoughts. And BOOM, before you know it, you're caged. EVERY DAY! This is what fear bondage is like. The adversary literally corners you in the same spiritual location – *deceit*. He begins to bombard you with lies and tells you, "You can't," "You're not smart enough," "You're going to fail," "No one loves you," "No one will ever love you," and so on. Again, THE DEVIL IS A LIAR! Rebuke all these thoughts right along with me even now.

> *Devil, you are a liar; I am a child of almighty God. I rebuke you and reject every lie you have told me in Jesus' Name. I send you, your lies, and all your evil deceptive ways back to the pits of hell, from whence they came. God is with me. God loves me. I belong to God. God is here. God has always been here. God will never leave me. God will never forsake me. Now, be gone.*

There's something about going through a tough time and feeling misunderstood. It's as if nothing is going right, and when you feel the warmth of the sunshine on your face, it's but for a few moments before fear flies in to rob you of your joy. Before you know it, you're pondering thoughts of *how soon will something bad happen again*? Because surely the good you feel *can't* last forever. Right? Such a state of *oh so subtle* inner turmoil. But is it subtle? Maybe not as subtle as we'd like to think. The good news is you are not alone in this, no matter how you feel. God is present. God's Word attests that He is with you even in the deepest valley (*see Psalm 23:4*)! Trust God is walking with you even now. Trust God is holding your hand. Trust if you continue to hold on, Your Heavenly Father will walk you right through the darkness into your earthly promised land. *Just hang on in there*!

Pray This:

Dear Lord, God:

Thank you for Your precious daughter or son reading this even now. Father, I ask that You guide Your child continuously on Your righteous path. May she no longer believe the lies of the adversary. No matter how many times he's stumbled. Help her to know her life is valuable. Help him to see his brokenness is useful. Help her to know You've been with her every step of the way. And the same way You have never left or forsaken him, You never will. Please rebuild the confidence of Your child even now. Please restore Your child's faith this moment. Thank You for hearing our prayer, most gracious, Father. Father, we absolutely love You and lift Your name on high! In Jesus' Name, we pray. Amen.

BELIEVE IT! YES, YOU CAN BE PUT BACK TOGETHER AGAIN! GOD IS REPAIRING YOUR BROKEN SPIRIT EVEN NOW. BE MADE WHOLE TODAY! LET'S GET BACK TO WORK IN THE MIRROR CLEANING STUDY GUIDE. EXERCISE SEVEN IS GOING TO HELP YOU MAKE MAJOR SHIFTS!

STEP EIGHT:

Getting in Touch with Who God Says You Are So You Can Embrace Change and Be Who You Are

Devotional

Romans 8.18-21 NRSV –

I consider that the sufferings of this present time are not worth comparing with the glory about to be revealed to us. For the creation waits with eager longing for the revealing of the children of God; for the creation was subjected to futility, not of its own will but by the will of the one who subjected it, in hope that the creation itself will be set free from its bondage to decay and will obtain the freedom of the glory of the children of God.

Two years ago, I was blessed to speak before a large audience. At this Christian Conference, my best friends and I experienced a lot of blessed moments. As I am accustomed to, there were also challenges. The warfare against the assignment God brought me there to fulfill was evident. One moment preaches.

The Sunday of checkout, I arose very early in the morning to drive my friend to the airport. It was still dark out. Unfortunately, my charger went home with my husband the previous day. Thankfully, the conference was in the city where I live. So, my battery died just as I dropped my friend off. Our truck was having a gas gauge issue where you could not determine how much gas it needed. Sometimes it would show as empty with a full tank. Either way, Jerrell took the car home with the *broken air* conditioning so I could have air in the truck. Being preoccupied with the weekend's events, I never thought, for one moment, the car could be out of gas. Well, just as I pulled back onto the interstate, the wheels *stiffened*, and the truck *grunted*. I was out of gas! I couldn't believe it. I'm literally on a dark stretch of the interstate before 5 am on a Sunday and terrified!

Suddenly I saw the next exit up ahead, but I was unsure if I would make it. I'm telling you, I was on flat terrain with a disabled gas pedal. This means I had no momentum to reach the exit. Yet, somehow, I was *pushed there*! I'm convinced God sent angels as I felt the car coasting along. When I reached the exit, the road declined downhill and ended at a red light. I knew I could not hit the brakes; otherwise, I would not have been able to travel the remaining distance up an incline to the gas station. I rode through the red light, and thankfully no other cars were approaching. But I didn't have the momentum to steer up the hill, so I parked in the median.

I jumped out and ran to the gas station, trying to simultaneously discern who looked the most approachable. Surprisingly, there were a lot of people out! A few getting gas, a few hanging, and a few who appeared under the influence and impacted by homelessness. I slowly walked towards one man, and I could tell he looked apprehensive. I prayed my appearance was non-threatening. I tried to briefly explain my situation, to which he responded, "So what, you want to use my phone?" I replied, "Yes, please." I opted to call 511, the Hero line for Georgia's Roadside Assistance – though I feared they would only help me if I was broken down on the highway. And the operator confirmed this was true. The man looked annoyed, so I returned his phone. I then recognized a woman was in the vehicle with him, which may have been the cause for his demeanor.

Tears began to well up in my eyes. I tried to be vigilant and prayed simultaneously. All the while, a few of the people who seemed high and drunk began to circle around me. I then remembered, most gas stations have gas cans for purchase! And thankfully, I had my bank card, so I had money! *Isn't it something how if you panic, you can lose focus and forget the resources you have access to? Especially when feeling stuck?* I went inside and grabbed a can. After anxiously standing in line, I learned this two-gallon can was over $16.00. *Highway Robbery*, as the older generation says! I complained, and the clerk told me there was a one-gallon can for half the price. He then told me how to use it. I was in a hurry and tuned him out. Another mistake. Thinking he was *mansplaining*, and how hard could it be? I would soon find out I was wrong. Dallas Willard says, as told by John Ortberg in *Soul Keeping: Caring for the Most Important Part of You*, "Hurry is the great enemy of spiritual life in our day. You must ruthlessly eliminate hurry from your life."

As I exited the station, a few swarmed around me again. I saw a man watching me from afar, so I asked if he would look out for me as I pumped gas into the can. He agreed. I was so nervous I wasted some onto my hand. He then escorted me to the median to put the gas in my truck – though he seemed a bit apprehensive. Once we arrived, we had a lot of trouble enabling the safety mechanism on the spout so the gas would release. Whew! Eventually, I found a label and read the instructions to him; it finally worked by God's grace!

I was so eager, I nearly jumped into the truck to immediately drive home. He was like, "Hey don't you need some gas?" and I was like, "Oh shoot, you are absolutely right!" So, I drove to the pump and filled up, and then I was on my way.

Yes, my friend, perhaps you've experienced a scary moment or two you'd prefer to erase from memory like me. What we must remember, as our focus scripture stated, "our present troubles do not compare to the glory to be revealed". Remind yourself, daily if you must, God knit you together, and God knew you before He placed you in your mother's womb. (*See Psalm 139:13-16 and Jeremiah 1:5.*) I made it home to retrieve my phone, and I headed back to the city to pack my room as I listened to Mike Todd's sermon, *Marked* on Youtube and then stuck around for the conference's worship service. As a result, I was ushered near the front and seated near a lady I bonded with after my session the day prior. She also purchased *Our Journey to #fertilityhope*. She was eager to re-connect with me, because I failed to sign her book, as we were focused in prayer. It may seem simple, but she let me know it was an answered prayer for her. I am proud to share she stayed connected with our ministry, and her daughter recently celebrated her first birthday! Won't God do it? Continue to press towards the mark of the high calling in Christ Jesus (Philippians 3:14). He will never fail you!

A Peek through My Window

Many leaders battle an over-achiever within. I am most certainly one who has faced this struggle. My nature to achieve developed in childhood. As mentioned in a previous chapter, my southern Black grandparents were college graduates. They were also church leaders. This means I learned academic achievement was important in my family at an early age. I also learned it was a great way to receive praise – particularly from my grandmother. Frankly, once I reached a certain age, my mother just expected me to excel.

The thing about working for praise – even as a certified school psychologist trained to recommend praise as a positive intervention for children with behavior issues, I realize it can become addictive for some children of certain wills. Once addicted, the child can be fueled to seek validation continuously. This seeking can pour into all achievement categories – be them academic/career-driven, personal image-related, and even in matters of spirituality. And validation can continuously be sought out – even as the child develops from adolescence into adulthood. Still, *In Becoming A Person of Influence*, Maxwell and Dornan say, "When a person feels encouraged, he can face the impossible and overcome incredible adversity." Can you relate? Who doesn't want to be encouraged?

It's evident all natural things require balance and order. Something good for you can become bad if over-indulged. Something that falls within a neutral category may also become maladaptive if over-used. What can we do to prevent such occurrences? Pay attention to what drives you. Pay attention at all times. *Be present.* Be present in all moments as they occur. Be in tune with your body. Be in tune with your thoughts. Be in tune with your spirit, as it connects with God's Holy Spirit. As a Spirit-led leader, if you find yourself on a continuous self-serving pattern, it's time to pause and check yourself.

Today I experienced my first meditations, guided by the Calm App. Today's Daily Calm focused on *the Gap*.[6] Being new to actively participating in mindful practices like meditation (*though in my field it is a widely recommended tool, the irony - I know*), I was also newly exposed to *the Gap*. *The Gap* is the natural pause which occurs between two events. Whether we always pay attention to it or not, there is always a pause.

Just the other day, I felt myself zooming from one task to the next as I was trying to shift from tending to each of my children's individual needs and quickly shift back to work and something stopped me dead in my tracks, just before sitting back down at my desk. I literally heard *pause* in my spirit. This pause was healthy. This pause was my reminder to slow down. This pause reminded me today has enough concerns for itself, and I should leave tomorrow's concerns where they belong ... the next day. As I paused for a brief moment, I realized the lists we create for ourselves, including God-led things, will always continue. As long as we have breath in our bodies, there will always be something to do. There will always be things to maintain. There will always be people and situations vying for our attention. Even as I'm writing, my daughter re-entered my office (*well after bedtime*) because she wanted me, and a pause is required.

(pause)

May this intentionally placed *pause* remind you *to pause* is necessary. For the pause is a break. The pause is a place to refuel. A pause is where we can rejuvenate ourselves, check in and remind ourselves why we are doing what we are doing. And if what we are doing is not ultimately serving God (*even rest serves God*), then it's time we stopped to evaluate. PAUSE. It's blessed. It's healthy. God is present in the pause.

The only way to truly tap into who God says you are, so you can embrace change and be who you are is through the pause. The pause is not a dirty word. Our chapter focus scripture ends by declaring we, "the creation of God be set free from bondage so we might obtain the freedom of the glory of the children of God" instead. Essentially, once we accept who God says we are, we may then walk into the fullness of becoming just that.

Pray This:

Father God, thank You for meeting your children here at step eight. Lord, thank You for teaching us how to re-align our spirits with Your Spirit. For You alone have made us a part of Your glorious creation, and You alone have declared us to be the children of God. Help us to walk into the full essence of who You desire for us to be. Give us the strength to pause, stop, wait, listen and discern what's next. Mighty God, we lift Your name on high. In Jesus' Name, we pray. Amen.

WOW! LOOK AT YOU DOING THE WORK! AND STILL, THERE'S MORE. HEAD ON OVER TO THE MIRROR CLEANING STUDY GUIDE TO COMPLETE EXERCISE EIGHT. YOUR BREAKTHROUGH IS JUST ON THE HORIZON.

STEP NINE:

Being Beyond Recognition is A Good Thing Because God is Doing A New Thing

Devotional

Romans 8.22-25 NRSV –

We know that the whole creation has been groaning in labor pains until now; and not only the creation, but we ourselves, who have the first fruits of the Spirit, groan inwardly while we wait for adoption, the redemption of our bodies. For in hope we were saved. Now hope that is seen is not hope. For who hopes for what is seen? But if we hope for what we do not see, we wait for it with patience. Who hopes for what is seen?

Who hopes for what is seen? Excellent question. Specifically, who hopes for what is seen amongst their personal possessions? It reminds me of how we desperately long for change in our lives. We pray repeatedly for the same thing over and over. We lie in bed awake at night, hoping God hears and will grant our requests soon. Then some time passes, and the new season comes. The very season you were desperate for! But how soon does the luster of the *brand new* fade? So soon ... I'm ashamed to think on it. But thankfully, we serve a gracious and compassionate God. A God who is gentle and takes time to cultivate us into being and becoming who He desires. A God who shapes us until we understand how to hope for what is *presently* unseen and do so with patience.

Today, I went home-shopping with a friend. My friend is ready to move out her condo and into a house. As a wise investor, she is searching for a home with a basement that can serve as rental income for potential tenants. If you know anything about fixer-uppers, it takes someone with vision to see what *could* be. To possess the imagination and the faith to believe in the potential opportunity of what lies before them – no matter how bleak the present circumstance appears.

Think with me. We have just approached a property and immediately noticed the siding installation ended at just about halfway down the side of the home. There are cinder blocks exposed on the bottom. Painted a different color than the top portion. On the same side of the house is a partially painted fence – in contrast to the other sections of fencing in the front and on the opposite side of the home. The yard is unmanicured. And when we arrive a thunderstorm breaks out, so we make a run for the door! Question - if this were your predicament, would you have enough hope to *search through* the opportunity in front of you? Would you have the patience? Or do you opt to remain in the car and drive off because, surely, nothing good could follow such ugly curb appeal?

As the focus scripture of this chapter states, "Now hope that is seen is not hope. For who hopes for what is seen? But if we hope for what we do not see, we wait for it with patience." Sometimes it takes a whole lot of hope to walk through the next phase of the journey. Especially when it doesn't look like what we expected upon arrival. Just like the rehab mentioned above was beyond recognition from its initial or desired state and something new was soon to be revealed. Trust, though you may not recognize yourself or what is happening during this season, God is still doing something new!

A Peek through My Window

I fell in love with Jesus a long time ago. I was exposed to ministry at a young age in a specific denomination. Because of my faithfulness, it took some time for me to grasp God's calling for me to do a *new thing*. The first struggle was in the fight to experience church beyond my roots. In my young adulthood, I was privileged to experience various styles of Christian worship at different churches. And then, when God called me to seminary, it seemed like such an inconvenient time for me vocationally, I put it off for another year. And during my delayed time, I experienced numerous hurdles. Some, in the profession I'd studied for up until that point. Others with my body being unable to produce children. The tests got to be so much until I felt compelled to apply and *secretly* hoped I wouldn't get in. I planned to tell God, "See, I tried, but it just didn't work." The process was seamless. Transcripts were turned around quickly. Recommenders did not hesitate to send their letters. None of them asked for an explanation regarding my *career shift*. And, though without funding, I got in. It was said there was no money left by the time I applied.

The school I applied for was one I presented at as part of a research team during my prior graduate studies. God reminded me of this memory. I was welcomed in, and I felt at home. I did not feel called to pulpit ministry, but I never wanted my access to preaching in certain spaces to be restricted, so I considered ordination. I even returned to my home denomination to fulfill a class requirement. I then thought I'd stick around to *see how it goes* and hopefully somehow, *haphazardly*, land myself on an ordination track. I gained friends and some foes. My perspective was broadened on various parts of life. My career was jeopardized, and I was forced to walk away while three months pregnant with my firstborn. But I kept going. I thought to myself, surely, I will finish what I've started, especially when I've sacrificed much to make it happen. Shockingly, while I was on the brink of planning strategic ways to load my schedule in preparation for my third and final year, I ran out of money. So, I cried and prayed and walked with my dear friend, Ruth, until we stumbled upon a park bench on the opposite side of campus. We stopped there together to pray. It was then God informed me He was calling me *away* from seminary. This was shortly after I launched my first stage production. I was planning to pursue my other creative endeavors while completing my Master of Divinity. I was shocked and astonished. I did not understand. But I was confident when the familiar peace of God's presence came over me as the Holy Spirit revealed what was required of me next. By that time, I had already given birth to Justice. My professors were understanding and accommodating to my being *mother*, it all seemed to work. Having experienced the voice of God calling me to move before, without hesitation, I unenrolled.

I gained a lot of *can-do* in seminary. I faced a lot of pain during the year just prior and the years following, but God allowed me to face my fears head-on. God propelled me forward in pursuing the many facets He created within me. God pushed me towards purposeful movement in my life. After which point, I returned home full-time, where I took care of Justice and pursued my publishing, ghostwriting and editing business. I expanded the Fertility Hope Ministry and Good People Great Things Magazine. I produced my stage play, 2 Sides, for the second year in a row, gave birth to my daughter, Broughton, and my son, Josiah. I even took a temporary gig or two here and there.

Suppose God used my seminary journey simply to slow me down. If so, it wouldn't be the last time. Afterall, while there I would give birth to my firstborn. It was also there where I would develop courage to persevere into being every part of the woman God has called me to be, in every area of my life. It was there I would push past fear to show my diverse gifts and talents, even while misunderstood.

It was clear my journey would be different from what I knew as ministry growing up, and it would not serve me well to compare my journey to others. Like a caterpillar going through metamorphosis in a cocoon, I was beyond recognition to most who knew me. My birth and marital families were perplexed, and my best friends were on the edge of their seats, praying I wouldn't fall as the next phase of who I was *becoming* unfolded.

After leaving seminary, I attempted to continue worship at the church where I served, but my husband was not happy. Thankfully, by that phase in my marriage, I knew the importance of not forcing or trying to force my spouse into doing something he disagreed with. *I'll tell you more when God calls me to speak on marriage.* So, we left shortly after Broughton's birth. The irony for our family is most of our church shifts occurred with the birth of a new child. Not exactly sure why. But I know each childbirth marks a transition, and God also couples *shifts* in multiple areas of our lives when our children are being born. Following, we attended church in a majority White congregation. I did not attempt to serve in the pulpit ministry, but I did minister. It felt good to breathe and hold hands for a moment while our children were in church childcare. Eventually, I joined small groups, which led to my serving as a small group leader and becoming connected with other leaders in the church. Sometime during my pregnancy with Josiah, our youngest child, we felt called away from this congregation too. Following, we felt called to return to the congregation where Jerrell and I first attended church together, which was under new leadership. As mentioned prior, while pregnant with Josiah, we held our first Fertility Hope Conference. *This is ministry.* Many were blessed during this conference, and many connected to this ministry have birthed babies.

A few months following Josiah's birth, the Holy Spirit called me to return to my former profession. After leaving to complete seminary, I honestly never saw myself returning. I now believe God took the taste out my mouth so I would focus on birthing my babies and other projects until it was time for me to return. I applied the Friday just before Winter Break, and I was hired in March. I went to work face-to-face for a week just prior to the shutdown due to the Covid-19 pandemic. And I love my job! It is a lot of work, but by implementing the skills I gained during my time away and maturing, I have better boundaries in place. This affords me the ability to serve as wife, mother, minister, school psychologist, and business owner. I no longer see my talents in one area as canceling the other talents I have. I now understand everything has its place and time. I also acknowledge I am still a work in progress. I now understand ministry happens across various avenues, and I must simply pay attention to when and how God wants me to operate. I also understand God has taken time to hold my hand to walk me through identifying my gifts and talents, and He allows me to choose different vehicles to operate them through. And there are still other times when God calls me to build and create specific vehicles to drive for specific seasons and particular purposes.

Listening is key. Discerning is key. Knowing scripture is key. Spending time with God daily is key. Reconnecting with God throughout the day is key. Establishing boundaries is key. Maintaining boundaries is key. Understanding positive boundaries let good stuff in and bad stuff out is key (Cloud & Townsend). Remember God is with you through it all. Remember being beyond recognition is a *good thing* because God is doing a *new thing*. If you seem unrecognizable to yourself and/or others, likely you are in a transitional period. If you don't understand, grab hold to God's hand even tighter and pursue what He has revealed for Your hands to do right now in this moment. Don't second guess the direction you are receiving if it doesn't line up with your expectations. Test the Spirit. When you receive God's confirmation, keep going.

Pray This:

Father God,

Thank You for giving your children the wherewithal to push through to step nine. Thank You for the reminder that it is okay to be beyond recognition sometimes. Thank you for walking with us and the reminder that You are doing a new thing! Thank You, Lord, for the reminder that we are to live for You and not for others. As we listen, discern and follow Your will, we offer the high praise You deserve. Thank You for Your amazing love! You are Mighty! You are Worthy of the Glory, the honor, and the praise! In Jesus' Name, we pray. Amen.

CAN YOU HARDLY BELIEVE YOU HAVE ALMOST REACHED THE END? HERE'S TO MAKING EVERY MOMENT COUNT. LET'S PRESS A LITTLE MORE. HEAD OVER TO THE MIRROR CLEANING STUDY GUIDE TO COMPLETE THE WORK IN EXERCISE NINE. SAY ALOUD, "I'VE GOT THIS!"

STEP TEN:

10 Habits to Help You Embrace Loving Your New Reflection

Devotional

Romans 8.26-32 NRSV –

Likewise the Spirit helps us in our weakness; for we do not know how to pray as we ought, but that very Spirit intercedes with sighs too deep for words. And God, who searches the heart, knows what is the mind of the Spirit, because the Spirit intercedes for the saints according to the will of God. We know that all things work together for good for those who love God, who are called according to his purpose. For those whom he foreknew he also predestined to be conformed to the image of his Son, in order that he might be the firstborn within a large family. And those whom he predestined he also called; and those whom he called he also justified; and those whom he justified he also glorified. What then are we to say about these things? If God is for us, who is against us? He who did not withhold his own Son, but gave him up for all of us, will he not with him also give us everything else?

What a powerful scripture reference! May it remind you of the presence of God. May it remind you of God's power, which is stronger than any force you will ever encounter. May it remind you not to focus on your weakness but focus on God's strength. May it remind you God knew you first. May it remind you the Holy Spirit's presence is real! May it remind you, in the great words of my deceased former Bishop Eddie L. Long, "If it ain't good yet, that means it's not over." May it remind you your life is not some random occurrence. May it remind you by God's design, it is impossible for you to have been smuggled into the earth. May it remind you, you are never alone, and you are a part of God's royal family. May it remind you God vouched for you before you were even born. May it remind you your life was not a practice run, but it is, in fact, *glorious, to the Glory of God*! May you forever be reminded God sacrificed His only son, a KING named Jesus so you might have life and have it to the full! Knowing this is where I leave you, it is important that I leave you with a few things. May these ten habits take you from *broken* to LEADER. Leave all doubt behind as you turn this book's final few pages.

A Peek through My Window

There is something very important I have come to know on my journey with Jesus. The people of God must understand the necessity of practicing spiritual habits alongside physical habits in the natural. Both are required to see the full manifestation of God's purpose(s) for their lives. With this, I implore you to not only read but execute the following as you press forward to embrace loving your new reflection. The truth is many may resolve to living a lifestyle of prayer alone (*without execution of their callings*) due to fear. Hear me well *(and then go do)*. It takes faith to walk out your prayers and passionately pursue purpose. It takes faith to believe God enough to trust God to work through you. It takes faith to listen and adjust as God prompts, understanding every purpose is for a particular time. It takes faith to move and not miss the moments. It takes faith to push past familiar patterns, especially when *familial*. As you navigate the new terrain God has placed before you, keep the following handy:

1) Pray and prepare.

2) Go to counseling.

3) Embrace the friends who walk with you season by season.

4) Do the work. Follow the process, follow the system.

5) Learn to reject, rebuke, and refute fear.

6) Always obey God: Your gifts will make room for you, and you will save time in doing so.

7) Take responsibility for your actions and understand there are always consequences for every choice.

8) Pay attention to the signs – if it walks like a duck and talks like a duck, it *usually is*.

9) Listen to God's instructions *the first time*.

10) Never doubt your capability or *your will* to carry out what God has created you to do.

* Bonus *

Most importantly, Plead the Blood of Jesus over all God has given you charge over each and every day of your life.

Pray This:

Lord God, thank You for making this reader completely whole in Jesus' Name! May she never again doubt the fullness of who you've designed her to be. May he quickly recognize Satan's lies no matter when he hears them going forward. May she execute rebuking and rejecting things that are not like You in Jesus' Name. May he fully understand and embrace the practice of refuting fear whenever it arises in his belly. May she stand tall and mighty as the lion placed within, ready to conquer all according to Your divine will and purpose for her life. May each recognize the beauty in brokenness, understanding they are better leaders because of their journey. I plead the Blood of Jesus over all. In Jesus' Name, we pray.

Amen.

TAKE THESE STEPS AND LEARN HOW TO LOVE THE ONE LOOKING AT YOU IN THE MIRROR. YOU WERE MADE IN THE IMAGE OF THE ALMIGHTY AFTER ALL. IT IS TIME FOR YOU TO LEAD. GO LEAD, *LEADER*.

HEAD OVER TO YOUR FINAL EXERCISE IN THE *MIRROR CLEANING* STUDY GUIDE. IT'S TIME TO EXECUTE EVERYTHING GOD HAS PLANTED IN YOUR HEART YOU HAVE BURIED FOR YEARS. NO MORE FEAR. NO HOLDING BACK. TURNS OUT THE EARTH NEEDS YOUR GIFTS. GO *LEADER*, FOR YOU ARE BROKEN NO MORE!

YOU WERE BORN TO LEAD!

EPILOGUE

Holding onto A Promise

Seasons have to change. – Felicia Renner

So, my Mom has exquisite taste. Her eye for art and furniture gravitates to things more ornate versus plain. She also happens to like larger pieces of furniture. For years she has collected furniture, art, and other decor from her various travels around the world. And for years, some of those beautiful pieces were hidden inside her gigantic armoires. Yes, tucked away. Inside the *big cabinets*. Where no light touched them.

When family would visit, myself included, we would question why she was collecting all these things. Her response, "They're for my new house!" We would look at her puzzled and say things like, "Less is more," "You should let go of some of these things," "Don't be weighed down by things," … You get the point. And she continued to maintain her stance. There were even rusted family heirlooms in the garage she declared would be refurbished in the future as we questioned this because of how much time had passed.

Well, as God would have it, my Mom had a new home constructed in the middle of the Covid-19 pandemic - *the home of her dreams*! With room for her grandkids, access to a country club, golf course, lake, and more! You see, as mentioned earlier, my mother is a divorcée without a co-parent. As in, she fought, scrapped, and scraped, with support from her birth family and others, to take care of my brother and me. This meant a lot of *sacrifice*. A lot of *delays*. A lot of *pain*. And a lot of "*one days*." And while her prior home served her and us well since I entered high school, her season there had long been overdue its finale. *And it was time for her to go*!

Thank God delay is not denial. She is now walking in her blessed place. Enjoying the fruits of her labor. She persevered even when misunderstood. She held onto God's promises for her life even when others thought she was crazy. And because of her steadfastness, she is in her beautiful new home surrounded by the beauty of God's promises fulfilled. It has been wonderful to witness her journey.

Now envision what your life can be like in the future as you continue to hold onto God's promises. I know you've seen many tough times, and life can get really scary, but rest assured, you are never alone, nor will you ever be. God has always been here, and God is here even now. Hang on in there.

Leader, it is time for you to come on out. Fly now. Now, fly!

ACKNOWLEDGMENTS

To God for the Call. To my dearest husband, Jerrell, thank you for always supporting me and our beautiful children whose bright smiles are a constant source of inspiration. To Jason, Courtney, Kendra & Travis, Felicia & Korch, Morgan, Jennifer, Kim, Charlene, Crystal, Angela, Chanyel, Ruth, Marquita, Lisa, and Candice and their families. You've all kept the torch lit for *Broken Leader* to propel me forward in seeing this book through execution after years of sitting on the idea of this publication. To Altimese for our talks and prayers and your support, my friend and owner of The Ezer Agency - responsible for PR & Marketing of this project. To Michaela for edits. To my mother, Wilma, for birthing and raising me, father, Rickey, for what he gave, my brothers and sisters, Rickey, Jr., Tammy, Ricardo, Amber, Phillip and others for our talks & your encouragement. To my grandmother, Wilhelmenia, who is a second mother, my other grandparents who have gone to be with The Lord, and their part in shaping who I've become. To my aunt, Yvette, who has always provided wise counsel. To my uncle, Dennis, for providing some of my earliest platforms for speaking and aunt, Wendy, for encouraging me in my youth. All cousins, aunts and uncles, here and in heaven. To my Thompson Family for your embrace. To my church mothers and fathers, and my teachers. To Grandpa Don for your timely wisdom. To my oldest friend, Ebony and her family, who have always accepted my rawest, funniest and brilliant self. To my counselor, Sanona, for helping to bring clarity to my thoughts around past pain. Thank you all family and friends and everyone else who has loved me and prayed for me inspite of my flaws; I love you. God's continued tremendous blessings over your lives, my fellow *Leaders*!

1. Pugh, Sullivan. May the Work I've Done Speak for Me. Excellence Music, 1977, Accessed August 1, 2020. https://hymnary.org/text/may_the_work_ve_done_speak_for_me.

2. Wright, Timothy. Trouble Don't Last Always. Savoy Records, 2009, Accessed August 1, 2020. https://www.lyrics.com/lyric/1173752/Rev.+Timothy+Wright/Trouble+Don%27t+Last+Always.

3. Tulsa Historical Society and Museum, Accessed June 15, 2021. https://www.tulsahistory.org/exhibit/1921-tulsa-race-massacre/

4. John Gray, interview by Steven Furtick, Become The Bridge | A Conversation With Pastor Steven Furtick & Pastor John Gray | Elevation Church, May 31, 2020. https://youtu.be/D7jTUfNyPkE

5. Attridge, Harold W. 2006. HarperCollins Study Bible. New York, NY: HarperOne.

6. Levitt, Tamara. Daily Calm App – The Gap

www.ingramcontent.com/pod-product-compliance
Lightning Source LLC
Chambersburg PA
CBHW071222160426
43196CB00012B/2385